Marcia Layton Turner

HarperCollins
Leadership

An Imprint of HarperCollins

THE DOMINO'S STORY

How the Innovative Pizza Giant Used
Technology to Deliver a Customer
Experience Revolution

© 2020 HarperCollins Leadership

Published by HarperCollins Leadership, an imprint of HarperCollins Focus LLC.

Published in association with Kevin Anderson & Associates: https://www.ka-writing.com/.

Book design by Aubrey Khan, Neuwirth & Associates.

ISBN 978-1-4002-1880-6 (eBook)
ISBN 978-1-4002-1879-0 (HC)

Library of Congress Control Number: 2020943544

Printed in the United States of America
20 21 22 23 LSC 10 9 8 7 6 5 4 3 2 1

For Domino's #1 fan, my daughter Amanda.

CONTENTS

ACKNOWLEDGMENTS

Without the help of skilled researcher Elizabeth King, there's no way this story could have been told in its entirety. Thanks also to Amanda Turner for her help with information gathering, to Sandy Beckwith for her eagle editing eye, to Domino's employee Kerstin for the frequent deliveries of a handmade pan pizza and eight-piece boneless chicken, to Jacob King for keeping the project on track, and Kevin Anderson for the opportunity to write this book.

1960

Dominick DeVarti sells DomiNick's pizzeria to brothers Tom and James Monaghan for around $900.

1965

Tom Monaghan renames the business Domino's Pizza, Inc.

1983

Domino's begins to expand internationally, opening up stores in Canada and Australia.

1990

Domino's acquires its 1,000th franchise.

1k

1998

Tom Monaghan sells Domino's to Bain Capital.

2004

Domino's becomes a publicly traded company on the New York Stock Exchange.

WALL ST

2007

For the ninth time, Domino's is ranked in the Top 10 on Entrepreneur magazine's annual list of great franchise opportunities.

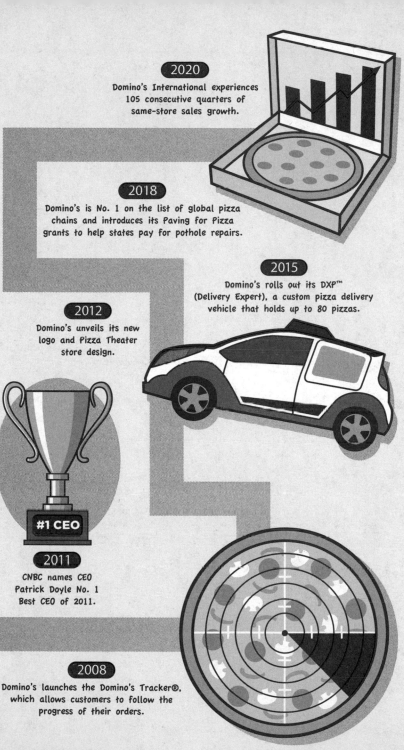

2020
Domino's International experiences 105 consecutive quarters of same-store sales growth.

2018
Domino's is No. 1 on the list of global pizza chains and introduces its Paving for Pizza grants to help states pay for pothole repairs.

2015
Domino's rolls out its DXP™ (Delivery Expert), a custom pizza delivery vehicle that holds up to 80 pizzas.

2012
Domino's unveils its new logo and Pizza Theater store design.

#1 CEO

2011
CNBC names CEO Patrick Doyle No. 1 Best CEO of 2011.

2008
Domino's launches the Domino's Tracker®, which allows customers to follow the progress of their orders.

INTRODUCTION

The story of Domino's Pizza is a true rags-to-riches tale, full of determination, innovation, and ambition. It involves a long-term vision for a business that would become a global corporate leader, creating jobs and supporting the local economy. In the present day, it includes a creative, technologically adept team committed to building a successful enterprise that has risen to the top of the charts for its industry.

The story begins with Thomas Stephen Monaghan, first son of Frank and Anna Monaghan, born in 1937. To understand how Domino's was founded and built, you first have to understand Tom Monaghan's upbringing and early experiences, because they shaped his goals and mind. A self-described "exuberant" child, full of energy, Monaghan's earliest memories are of life in Ann Arbor, with his brother, Jim, two years his junior; a patient, loving father; and a mother who was a good bit less patient, he relates in *Living the Faith*, a biography of his life.

What shaped his life perhaps more than anything else was the sudden death of his twenty-nine-year-old doting dad to peritonitis, due to ulcers. Even after a lump-sum payment from Frank's life insurance policy, Monaghan's mother could barely make ends meet. She moved her boys into town and got a job at the

Argus Camera Company, but with weekly earnings of $27.50 and expenses of $30, she knew she had to find a better solution.

That solution was to put her sons into a foster home. They first stayed briefly with one family before being moved for a two-year stint with the Woppmans. However, when Monaghan was around seven, the Woppmans decided he was just too much for them, and returned both boys to their mother.

Around that same time, Anna Monaghan decided to go back to school to become a nurse. Her plan was to place the boys in Catholic boarding school until she earned her degree, and then they would come live with her again when she was making enough money to afford their care. In the meantime, Tom and Jim Monaghan went to live and study at St. Joseph's Home for Boys, which was both a school and an orphanage.

Although he was "intensely unhappy about my strange new surroundings,"[1] he says, the light in the darkness was one nun who was uplifting. "Sister Berarda always encouraged me, even when my ideas seemed far-fetched," he says in the book. That included when he told his second-grade class that he was going to be a priest, an architect, *and* shortstop for the Detroit Tigers. Although his classmates laughed, Sister Berarda assured him, "I don't think it's ever been done before, Tommy, but if you want to, there's no reason you can't."[2] And with that, it's likely Monaghan decided he would do just that.

On reflecting on her influence, Monaghan acknowledged how important that relationship had been. "She became my surrogate mother, and I flourished under her care." His own mother worked at the hospital a few blocks away and had an apartment close by, so the boys often visited on weekends, Monaghan recalls. While he excelled in second grade with Sister Berarda's support, when he and Jim were transferred to the local Catholic school in third grade, things took a turn for the worse. The environment was harsh, with whippings common for the smallest infraction, he says, and his grades and attitude fell during his time there. Yet, during those four years, he also says he learned the value of hard work and of not giving up. "If something doesn't work, you try another way. You can't fail." Those teachings certainly served Monaghan well later at Domino's.

> He told his second-grade class that he was going to be a priest, an architect, *and* shortstop for the Detroit Tigers. Although his classmates laughed, Sister Beranda assured him, "I don't think it's ever been done before, Tommy, but if you want to, there's no reason you can't."

Back Together

Finally, when Monaghan was in sixth grade, Anna Monaghan took the boys from St. Joseph's and moved north to Traverse City, Michigan, where she had a job and had bought a house. Suddenly, Monaghan had more freedom than he'd ever experienced, since his mother worked long hours at the hospital. In seventh grade, he enrolled at Immaculate Conception Catholic school and then spent his summer working to earn money through odd jobs. He had already figured out that money was critical to having more freedom, so he sold papers downtown and then vegetables door-to-door to earn some cash.

But after returning from a visit to Monaghan's aunt and uncle's place in Ann Arbor that summer, Anna decided she just couldn't handle him anymore, so she once again placed her sons in foster care. In and out of a few families, when Monaghan began ninth grade at St. Francis High School, he was sent to live on a farm and his brother went back to live with their mother. One of Monaghan's jobs on the farm netted him a paycheck of $2 a week, which he was thrilled about. The house was drafty and he did his homework in the kitchen by the light of a kerosene lamp, then spent his free time reading catalogs, dreaming of the day that he would be able to afford the best of everything. He was going to be rich and famous, he told his friends. And they believed him.

However, he soon had a revelation, due in part to his desire to return to the rituals and routine he had become accustomed to at school. In his freshman year, he says in his book, "I saw that I had been wallowing in crass, worldly thoughts when I should have been concentrating on my spiritual quest. I decided then and there that I would become a priest."

With help, he applied to St. Joseph's Seminary in Grand Rapids, Michigan, and was accepted. He was thrilled, but he only lasted a year there, not due to poor conduct, but because his mother complained to the rector that he wasn't writing home enough. He admits that he didn't write to her as often as other kids wrote to their mothers, but he never would have thought that would get him kicked out of seminary. He was devastated at being asked to leave, and Anna was shocked that her letter had brought him back to her. She hadn't bargained on that.

After another stint in a foster home, Anna had him remanded to a juvenile detention center, until Monaghan's aunt found out and effectively bailed him out, bringing him home with her to Ann Arbor. He says his time with them was the first time since his father's death that he was leading a normal life.

Although he was known for having "grandiose ideas," Monaghan was not invested in his schoolwork. He was more interested in working at local jobs, where he challenged himself to be the best at whatever role he was playing: soda jerk, bowling pin setter, or busboy. Because of his low grades, he didn't bother applying to college, choosing instead to get an apartment and work at a newspaper distributor. Once he had saved up enough money, he applied to the newly opened Ferris State College and was admitted. After his freshman year, his grades were good enough to be admitted to the University of Michigan. But he had no money for tuition, so he joined the military, where he was assigned to the Marine Corps. During his time in the service, he read self-improvement books voraciously.

After being honorably discharged, he went back to Ann Arbor and again got a job with the newspaper distributor. Only this time, the owner taught him the business and Monaghan proved skilled at working with the carriers. He saved his money and finally had enough to enroll at the University of Michigan but soon left after realizing he was in over his head in most of the subjects.

This is why when his mail carrier and part-time pizza deliveryperson brother Jim suggested that the two should buy a pizzeria named DomiNick's from its owner, Dominick DiVarti, Tom was game. In fact, he was more than game. He was all in. He saw the potential that the business had to become the start of his business empire—an empire that would eventually allow him to buy the Detroit Tigers. Monaghan wasn't wrong.

As you'll read in the following chapters, through hard work, curiosity, investment in technology, and a focus on customer satisfaction, Monaghan built a business that is still thriving and growing today, more than sixty years later. But Monaghan wasn't just in the right place at the right time. He applied common sense and sound business practices—practices you'll read about and have the opportunity to apply to your own organizations—to establish and grow a global enterprise.

> " Through hard work, curiosity, investment in technology, and a focus on customer satisfaction, Monaghan built a business that is still thriving and growing today, more than sixty years later.

"The secret of good pizza is in the sauce. . . . That made a lasting impression on me. I vowed right then that I would have the best pizza sauce in the world."

—TOM MONAGHAN

CHAPTER ONE

DOMINICK'S, DOMINO'S PREDECESSOR

Pizza in all its forms—fresh, frozen, parbaked, stuffed, round, square, thin crust, thick crust, cauliflower crust, gluten-free—continues to account for an ever-increasing portion of consumer meal budgets. Globally, pizza is a $155 billion industry that grew 4.6 percent between 2019 and 2020, reports *PMQ Pizza Magazine*'s "Pizza Power Report 2020."[1] Consumer demand for convenient meals is one reason pizza remains a staple of most American diets, although preference for the dish continues to rise in other parts of the world. But it's no surprise that consumer love for the dough-tomato-sauce-cheese combo is expected to remain strong for years to come.

Yet 2019 was a turning point for one pizza chain in particular: Domino's. That was the year that Domino's Pizza finally claimed the number one spot in total sales—a spot that Pizza Hut had long held. Domino's sales increased 8.3 percent in global retail sales and the chain added 232 net stores during the third quarter of 2018 alone.

> " Domino's Pizza finally claimed the number
> one spot in total sales—a spot that Pizza
> Hut had long held. Domino's sales increased
> 8.3 percent in global retail sales and the
> chain added 232 net stores during the third
> quarter of 2018 alone.

There are a number of reasons for the sales surge, from an improved pizza recipe to rising investments in technology, including a realization of the importance of mobile as a sales channel, to a commitment to not just satisfying customers, but delighting them. Making ordering possible from nearly any platform was a big step forward. Today, Domino's is the largest pizza operation in the world. It only took sixty years to get to that point.

Humble Beginnings

Although a massive company today, Domino's Pizza began as a small pizza shop in Ypsilanti, Michigan, a suburb of Ann Arbor. Back in 1960, Dominick DeVarti, an Ann Arbor restaurateur, opened DomiNick's doors, according to *Franchising in America*, with locations in Ypsilanti and two in Ann Arbor. It was not an immediate success and he quickly realized that he didn't have the time or patience to give to the shop. He shuttered it in order to focus on the Ann Arbor business. But when DeVarti's friend James "Jim" Monaghan overheard a conversation between DeVarti and a potential buyer about the closed pizzeria, Jim and his older brother, Tom, approached him about selling his shop. So, in December 1960, in exchange for around $900 in cash and an agreement to assume the store's debt, which was somewhere between $2,200 and $8,000, depending on who you ask, DeVarti handed over the keys to DomiNick's to the Monaghan men.

Despite the fact that DeVarti had struggled to make a go of the place, the Monaghans thought running a pizza shop would be a good investment. In fact, that was all Tom Monaghan had expected to be—an investor. Both brothers had visions of being able to staff the shop themselves in their spare time. It was a side hustle for Jim, who worked full-time at the post office. Tom's main goal was generating enough cash to cover the cost of his tuition at the University of Michigan, where he was a student.

Because DeVarti had only opened the shop between 5 p.m. and midnight each night, the Monaghans envisioned being able to juggle work or school and their pizza venture simultaneously. DeVarti allowed the Monaghans to continue to use the name DomiNick's and, in a fifteen-minute lesson, showed them how to make pizzas. Tom Monaghan recalls in *Living the Faith* that DeVarti told him, "The secret of good pizza is in the sauce." He says, "That made a lasting impression on me. I vowed right then that I would have the best pizza sauce in the world."[2]

Although the brothers made only $99 their first week in business, it was a start. It was also quite a feat since they had no phone service initially; the phone company demanded that they pay for the quarter-page ad that DeVarti had bought before the phone would be turned on. Although they wanted to refuse, the Monaghans understood the importance of the phone line. They paid the bill.

At first, the brothers had no problem with the nightly schedule. And as they expanded the pizza shop's hours, business also picked up. By June, the duo was reportedly earning about $400 a week in profits. That number quickly dropped, however, when students at Eastern Michigan University (EMU), which was across the street, left campus for the summer. That's also when Jim accepted the reality that running a pizza shop was a poor choice for a side job. Eight months in, he sold his share of the business to Tom in exchange for ownership of the shop's 1959 Volkswagen Beetle, which they had been using for deliveries.

> DeVarti told him, "The secret of good pizza is in the sauce." He says, "That made a lasting impression on me. I vowed right then that I would have the best pizza sauce in the world."

Tom stepped up his involvement in the business after Jim's departure and was soon faced with a decision: the shop needed more of his time and attention to be profitable, but he couldn't give that and still go to college full-time. He had to choose. Seeing the business's potential, he opted to drop out of the University of Michigan in 1961 to devote himself to DomiNick's.

Rather than feeling conflicted about his decision, Monaghan is reported to have said, "In that instant, I made the decision to commit myself heart and soul to being a pizza man. And I felt a tremendous sense of relief."

When he wasn't working in the shop, Monaghan was conducting market research. He apparently sampled the pizza at nearly every restaurant in Ypsilanti and Ann Arbor, taking careful notes of each pie's pros and cons. He wanted to be sure DomiNick's had the best pizza sauce around. During a conversation with a supplier one day, the supplier told him the best pizza sauce *he'd* ever had was at an old Italian restaurant in Lansing. So Monaghan took a drive to Lansing to taste for himself, ultimately agreeing that it was the best sauce he'd ever tasted too. He complimented the owner, who promptly took him into the kitchen and showed him how to make it.

Armed with a delicious sauce, DomiNick's sales rose to $750 per week by April 1962, but dropped again to around $200 a week when the semester ended. During the summer, Monaghan used his free time wisely, studying how to make the pizza operation more efficient. He knew he had a great product, so the next step was increasing profits. He was obsessed with improving the layout of the oven and the counters, he recalls in *Living the Faith*. Little by little, he shaved seconds and minutes off the time it took to prepare and bake a pizza, improving his bottom line incrementally with each adjustment. When the EMU fall semester started, the shop's revenues rose in concert, buoyed by Monaghan's decision to also simplify DomiNick's menu.

That decision actually came out of necessity, when, one Sunday night—DomiNick's busiest night because the dorms didn't serve meals that day—most of Monaghan's employees failed to show up. Half-staffed, Monaghan struggled with whether to open that night when someone suggested, "Why don't you just cut out the six-inch pizzas?" There were five sizes of pizzas on the menu, but the six-inch "took just as long to make as the big one and just as much time to deliver, but cost less," Monaghan explained to *Fortune Small Business*.[3] The shop got busy but not overwhelmingly so and sales rose 50 percent that night. "All of a sudden I was making money," he says. The next night, they nixed the nine-inch pizza and income from that night let him get caught up on his bills. "I learned then that keeping things simple could be more profitable," Monaghan says.

Feeling like the business was running smoothly, with two employees on the payroll at that point, Monaghan began considering opening other locations in college towns, such as in Mount Pleasant, Michigan, home to Central Michigan University's five thousand students. But realizing his precarious financial situation, Monaghan retreated. A conversation with a regular customer seemed to create another opportunity for him, however, when he discovered the regular was an Ann Arbor pizza legend—Jim Gilmore, founder of Pizza from the Prop, which was the first known pizzeria in the country to offer free delivery. Monaghan was enamored with his experience and, with some prodding, agreed to bring Gilmore in as a 50/50 partner, in exchange for a $500 buy-in that Gilmore would have to work off. Gilmore's attorney drew up the legal paperwork that, in hindsight, was clearly in Gilmore's favor, putting all future debts and obligations in Monaghan's name, since Gilmore's recent bankruptcy disqualified him from signing such a contract, the story went. Gilmore also let Monaghan know that he intended to keep his day job cooking in the University of Michigan dorms, but assured him it wouldn't interfere with pizza making.

The Business Grows

Soon thereafter, in 1962, Monaghan took Gilmore to Mount Pleasant to scout for a location for their next pizza shop. They found a tiny hole-in-the-wall in the back of a diner and set up shop after Monaghan shelled out $2,200 for a used oven, refrigerator, and a stainless-steel counter. Gilmore still owed the company $500 for his stake, but until that point had contributed only his expertise. Monaghan put him in charge of running the Ypsilanti shop so that Monaghan could focus on the new one.

The Mount Pleasant location opened its doors under the Pizza King brand, which Gilmore had suggested, serving the same great pizza as in Ypsilanti, also delivered for free, and sales quickly eclipsed the Ypsilanti location. In a matter of months, the two stores combined were generating $3,000 a week in sales.

Over the next few months, Monaghan became somewhat alarmed at Gilmore's frequent requests for money to support the now-struggling Ypsilanti location, where sales had declined by one-third. Gilmore told him he was working hard to upgrade it, but when Monaghan dropped in unexpectedly a few months later, he was shocked by the poor appearance of the shop and the poor taste of the pizzas. He wondered where the money was going because it surely hadn't been invested in the business.

After expressing his alarm and displeasure with Gilmore, Monaghan shifted gears to how to turn the situation around. In response, Gilmore told him about a great opportunity to open a third shop in Ann Arbor, just blocks from the University of Michigan's central campus. After seeing it, Monaghan agreed and sold half of his stake in the Mount Pleasant Pizza King for $4,000 to raise the needed funds to renovate and outfit the new shop with cooking equipment.

The new shop opened in May 1962 but didn't take off as the partners had expected. The Ypsilanti shop, which had moved to a new spot when the lease was up, was breaking new sales records, but Ann Arbor was languishing. Gilmore argued that they needed to expand the menu offerings, so Monaghan sold his remaining interest in the Mount Pleasant Pizza King for $4,000 and took on a third partner, local restaurateur Red Shelton, for another $4,000.

That was also the year that Monaghan married Marjorie Zybach, whom he had met when delivering pizzas to her dorm. The Monaghans lived in a trailer while he put in hundred-hour weeks building his business.

In 1963, Monaghan opened another pizza delivery location on the east side of Ypsilanti under the Pizza King name. "There wasn't enough room to do prep work, so he came up with a brilliant solution: do the prep work for both stores at the Cross Street location and drive supplies to the second location daily. Centralizing prep work, he recognized, would allow him to have smaller, more efficient stores focused exclusively on making and delivering pizza," James Leonard reports in *Living the Faith.*[4]

> " There wasn't enough room to do prep work, so he came up with a brilliant solution: do the prep work for both stores at the Cross Street location and drive supplies to the second location daily. Centralizing prep work, he recognized, would allow him to have smaller, more efficient stores focused exclusively on making and delivering pizza.

Sometime that year, Monaghan dropped in to see DeVarti in Ann Arbor and, discovering he wasn't in, spontaneously ended up pitching in to help make pizzas when a flurry of orders came in. The next day, when DeVarti heard about how Monaghan had shown off his pizza-flipping skills to DeVarti's customers, he was upset, apparently assuming that Monaghan was trying to poach customers. As a result, DeVarti told Monaghan that he no longer had permission to use the DomiNick's name, indicating that the name had been confusing to customers—especially after witnessing Monaghan behind DeVarti's counter—about whose restaurant was whose. Not wanting to suddenly change the shop's name, he complied—sort of. For the next year, Monaghan marketed his pizza shop as Ypsilanti DomiNick's, while he pondered what name to use instead.

At the end of 1963, the partners bought out Red Shelton's interest and, the next year, at Gilmore's urging, bought a full-sized restaurant for $90,000 and named it Gilmore's Restaurant. Much like Monaghan's other partnerships with Gilmore, it lost money from the start.

In 1965, Monaghan severed ties with Gilmore. The final straw in that partnership's history was when Monaghan discovered that while he and his wife were sacrificing for the business, working long hours and living in a trailer, his partner had been living large, spending more time making improvements to his large home than working at the pizza shop he had been responsible for.

He could now have a fresh start.

"Our growth was just a symptom of the franchise fever that was sweeping the nation at the time. McDonald's and Kentucky Fried Chicken were widely copied, and all kinds of celebrities . . . were lending their names to restaurant chains."

—TOM MONAGHAN

CHAPTER TWO

FRANCHISING BEGINS

Tom Monaghan's split with business partner Jim Gilmore in 1965 turned out to be the catalyst that unified his three differently branded pizzerias. It was the spark that led to the creation of Domino's Pizza, Inc. At the time, owning and managing three pizzerias with different names didn't make a whole lot of sense to Monaghan, who wanted to unite them all under one umbrella, one name. He turned to a local advertising agency for naming advice. Agency partner Sam Fine advised Monaghan to "use something as similar to DomiNick's as possible. People are used to DomiNick's, and when they look in the phone book for it, they'll find your name."[1]

Agreeing with Fine that his strategy made sense, Monaghan began brainstorming with employees to try and come up with a new name for the business. "We must have gone through hundreds of different names," he recalls in *Living the Faith*.[2] Then, one day, employee Jim Kennedy had an aha moment. Monaghan recalled to *Fortune Small Business*:

One day an employee came back from delivering a pizza and said, "I've got our name! Domino's!" I said, "That's great!" I'd never heard of a Domino's pizza before. It was Italian, and we could use a domino logo. I decided we'd put three dots on the domino because we had three stores, and every time we added one, we'd add a dot. You can see I wasn't thinking of a national chain back then.[3]

> **I'd never heard of a Domino's pizza before. It was Italian, and we could use a domino logo. I decided we'd put three dots on the domino because we had three stores, and every time we added one, we'd add a dot. You can see I wasn't thinking of a national chain back then.**

Kennedy's timing couldn't have been better, since Monaghan was under the gun to finalize a Yellow Pages ad.[4] Domino's Pizza, Inc. was born.

After renaming his enterprise, Monaghan turned his attention to franchising his pizza delivery concept. Franchising had gained considerable traction in the 1950s as industries like gas stations, fast-food restaurants, and car dealerships made franchising the dominant business model. Thomas Dicke, author of *Franchising in America: The Development of a Business Method, 1840–1980,* stated: "By the end of the 1960s it was used to sell virtually every type of good or service imaginable, and the franchise outlet had become a ubiquitous feature of the American landscape."[5] Virtually every industry was seeing the rise of franchises, from hotels and Holiday Inn and Sheraton, to convenience stores and 7-Eleven, automotive service and Midas Muffler, dry cleaning and Martinizing, and even home services, like Roto-Rooter plumbing[6] and, later, Stanley Steemer carpet cleaning.

By 1966, Pizza Hut already had 145 franchise units,[7] and in 1968, McDonald's already had its 1,000th location and was expanding internationally.[8]

The First Domino's Pizza Franchise

It was around this time that Monaghan started thinking seriously about franchising Domino's. He was doing all right financially with three stores, but "he wanted to do more than merely survive. He wanted to thrive, and he believed the way to do it was through franchising. Instead of selling a pizza, he would sell a concept—with a slice off the top for the concept's creator and owner," Leonard explains in *Living the Faith*.[9] So he began to explore what franchising would entail.

> He wanted to thrive, and he believed the way to do it was through franchising. Instead of selling a pizza, he would sell a concept—with a slice off the top for the concept's creator and owner

Monaghan told *Fortune Small Business*:

> In the late '60s, I attended a franchise seminar at Boston College, and that's when I started getting inspired. I met Ray Kroc [from McDonald's]. I met John Y. Brown from KFC. These guys flew in on their Lear jets and had their Rolls-Royces outside. I said, "Wow, what I've got with this concept of pizza delivery is just as good as what they have; I just don't have as many stores."[10]

He had a board of directors, which included Monaghan; his wife, Margie, who was also the company's bookkeeper; and his attorney, Larry Sperling, whom Monaghan relied on to help design a new franchise arrangement for Domino's. On the hunt for franchisees, Sperling suggested to Monaghan that local politician Chuck Gray might be a potential franchisee. When the two men met, Monaghan says that he was impressed with Gray and that his "enthusiasm for Domino's" was very appealing. As they worked out the franchise agreement, which included Monaghan personally training Gray in pizza-making, Monaghan saw that Gray "had a natural talent for the pizza business."[11] Gray would be Domino's first franchisee, buying the existing Domino's operation on the east side of Ypsilanti with no money down.

> "Sperling drafted a franchise agreement, which we signed on April 1, 1967. It gave us 2.5 percent of Gray's sales as a royalty, another 2 percent for advertising, and 1 percent for providing all his bookkeeping, from P&L statement to payroll, all of which was done by my wife. By today's standards, the royalties were far too favorable to the franchisee. But it served our purpose then, and I was not concerned about covering all future contingencies," Monaghan says in his book *Pizza Tiger*.[12]

As part of the deal, Gray also agreed to buy his supplies directly from Monaghan's commissary, both providing income to Domino's and helping to ensure that product quality across every location would be the same.

The first franchise was a success. "Sales went up after Gray took over and business doubled in a year," according to Monaghan in *Living the Faith*.[13] And Monaghan's fortunes started to swing in a positive direction. He went from owning three stores and being $90,000 in debt at the start of 1967 to having six stores, no debt, and $50,000 in profit by year-end.[14]

Domino's Franchising Takes Off

Buoyed by the success of the first franchise, Monaghan began looking for his next franchisee. He had had his eye on a current employee who he thought was ready to run his own show—Dean Jenkins. Next, he found a vacant building in Ann Arbor and leased it, with plans to build a Domino's storefront from the ground up. It was the first such location—built from scratch. It proved to be more challenging than Monaghan had anticipated, leading his construction team to scrounge up parts and improvise when a solution was needed. "Improvisation has grown into an operational style among our store-development people," says Monaghan. "Think fast, solve problems on the spot, and don't worry about finding out what caused any screw-ups until after you've got the store open," was the guiding principle in those days.[15] Improvise, find a solution, and forget about blaming.

Jenkins was Monaghan's pick to run the newly renovated shop as the second franchisee because of how meticulously he approached every task he was assigned. Although Jenkins's colleagues initially called him "Slow Motion," because of his slow, methodical pace, Monaghan worked with him to help him pick up his pace. It was his dream to run his own business and Monaghan wanted to make that happen for him.[16] The Ann Arbor shop was up and running by July 1967 and profitable almost immediately. It was at that point that Monaghan decided to try and capture some of the pizza market at Michigan State University in East Lansing.

"Monaghan made pizza boxes that were extra-durable and insulated. . . . It was a winning combination that directly led to his 30-minute guarantee roll-out in 1973, and within 10 years he was rich enough to buy the Detroit Tigers."

—MASHED

CHAPTER THREE

COLLEGE CAMPUSES BECOME HOME TURF

The decision to continue to expand the Domino's enterprise on college campuses was due in part to demand from college students for regular pizza deliveries and Monaghan's in-depth knowledge of that market. In *Pizza Tiger*, Monaghan claims that, in the late 1960s, "I knew, within 5 or 10 percent, the dorm capacity of every college in the country. I also knew the comparative breakdown at each school between men's dorms and women's (a lot more pizzas are ordered from men's dorms) as well as their total enrollment."[1] Monaghan's understanding of college student demographics and demand was certainly a competitive advantage for Domino's.

The other reason that college campuses were so appealing to Domino's, according to *The Advertising Age Encyclopedia of Advertising*, was the relative low cost of promotion: Domino's "could reach college students effectively and inexpensively through their college newspapers,"[2] rather than having to pay higher mainstream advertising rates to reach residential customers.

" I knew, within 5 or 10 percent, the dorm capacity of every college in the country. I also knew the comparative breakdown at each school between men's dorms and women's (a lot more pizzas are ordered from men's dorms) as well as their total enrollment." Monaghan's understanding of college student demographics and demand was certainly a competitive advantage for Domino's.

Early Franchisees

After selling a first franchise to Chuck Gray in Ann Arbor and a second to Dean Jenkins, who ran the first Domino's to be built from the ground up, Monaghan shifted his attention to introducing Domino's to another college town—"the big plum," Monaghan called it—East Lansing, home of Michigan State University. With approximately twenty thousand students living in dorms there, the potential market was quite appealing to the pizza purveyor. In fact, it was the largest college community in the country at that time.

Monaghan's attorney, Larry Sperling, was nervous about the expansion in to Lansing and some changes to the company's operations, which put the whole venture at risk if Monaghan's plans failed. Of course, Monaghan had no intention of failing, but he listened to Sperling and, consequently, created a new entity, Domino's of Lansing, Inc., as the owner of that shop. Monaghan was the sole shareholder.

What was exciting about East Lansing, besides the sheer size of the pizza-eating population, was a new commissary concept Monaghan had developed. He wanted to set up a central storehouse of ingredients and supplies at the East Lansing location that would serve the other stores in the area. He could buy raw materials in volume, netting lower purchase prices, and then provide what the stores in the chain needed through the commissary, helping to fund continued growth in the franchise system and help ensure the same quality across the board.

Monaghan also wanted to try culling his menu items, limiting pizza sizes to one: 12" pizzas. He reasoned that since 80 percent of all the orders from dorms were for the 12" size, why go to the trouble of selling other variations? If the customer wanted more pizza, they could simply order more than one 12" pie. Offering one size would make it possible to provide better quality pizzas, since pizza makers only needed to learn how to make one size, as well as faster service. Other advantages Monaghan identified were reducing errors and cost savings from only having to order one size delivery box.[3]

Already considering implementing a computer system for processing orders, Monaghan wanted to reduce the number of variables involved in pizza orders. In addition to offering only a 12" pizza, Domino's also reduced the number of topping choices to six. But after a negative response from the Lansing store employees, Monaghan added another size to the menu—a 16" pizza. The two sizes, small and large, would become Domino's standard menu items.

Calling the Lansing store "a hotbed of innovation,"[4] Monaghan credits Terry Voice, a young store manager who, like Monaghan, was always on the lookout for ways to make the operation more efficient. He developed the strip sub for taking pizza orders, replacing the old process involving copying orders from a sales slip onto the side of the pizza box. Voice's design had the phone order taker write the customer's order on a carbon-backed form that included the time the order came in, the customer's address and contact information, the order, and any extra information that would be helpful in finding the house. The original part of the two-part form was torn off and moved with the pizza as it was made and was then taped to the box for delivery. Having the order slip moving with the pizza helped ensure the order was correct and saved valuable minutes in the pizza prep process.

Lansing was also home to "Big Red," which was the world's largest pizza oven, able to hold up to ninety pizzas at a time. The oven had ten 12-foot-long Ferris-wheel trays that could hold at least nine 12-inch pizzas per tray. Monaghan described it as "like using a blast furnace to grill hamburgers"—overkill, at least at first. And, eventually, not big enough.

As he was developing and enhancing the Domino's franchise model, Monaghan was also on the hunt for more franchisee prospects. Dave Kilby, whom Monaghan had worked with as a radio copywriter and as a volunteer on the Junior Chamber of Commerce's pizza sale, ended up buying the old Pizza on the Prop location in Ann Arbor for $10,000, with no money down. Monaghan financed it and spent as much time training him in pizza making as he had with Gray, once Kilby decided he wanted to be part of the pizza company. Kilby became the in-house organizing guru when he wasn't managing his own store. Eventually, Monaghan gave him responsibility for managing all the store managers and gave him an office in the company's Ypsilanti headquarters.

> " Lansing was also home to "Big Red," which was the world's largest pizza oven, able to hold up to ninety pizzas at a time. The oven had ten 12-foot-long Ferris-wheel trays that could hold at least nine 12-inch pizzas per tray. Monaghan described it as "like using a blast furnace to grill hamburgers"—overkill, at least at first. And, eventually, not big enough.

Gene and Becky Belknap were the system's next franchisees, opening a shop on Ann Arbor's north side. Both had been Domino's employees, having met while working for the company. Their store opened in 1968 as part of a "no-money-down deal."[5]

Expanding beyond Michigan

Domino's first franchisee outside of Michigan was Steve Litwhiler, a former Ypsilanti Domino's delivery driver who headed to college at the University of Vermont and ended up staying in Burlington to teach. Only he wasn't enjoying it and "the pay is lousy,"[6] he told Monaghan during a phone call. Litwhiler reported that he had made more money as a Domino's pizza deliveryman and wanted to open a store in Burlington. Although Monaghan wasn't excited about opening a store so far from

Ypsilanti, he liked Litwhiler and was confident he would be successful. The Burlington store opened in 1968, followed by four more in the subsequent two years.[7]

By year-end 1968, Monaghan had twelve franchisees. His goal for the next twelve months was to open a new store every week. He had already scoped out six areas that he believed were ripe for Domino's development. Like the existing outlets, "Each area was built around a college or university, each had one or more campus stores to serve as anchors and two or more residential stores to sew up the market with a common commissary to supply them all."[8]

Although he didn't quite reach his goal of sixty-four stores by the end of 1969, he did have forty-two Domino's Pizza stores situated in three states: Michigan, Vermont, and Ohio. The pace of development did pick up in the 1970s and '80s. By 1978, Domino's had two hundred outlets, and by 1983, there were one thousand. And Monaghan had laid out a plan to set up franchisees at all the major college campuses in the Midwest, starting with Purdue University in Lafayette, Indiana.[9]

> " Although he didn't quite reach his goal of sixty-four stores by the end of 1969, he did have forty-two Domino's Pizza stores situated in three states: Michigan, Vermont, and Ohio. The pace of development did pick up in the 1970s and '80s. By 1978, Domino's had two hundred outlets, and by 1983, there were one thousand.

The system's expansion continued in Ohio, with another former driver from Ypsilanti, Lester Heddle, opening a store near Ohio University, in Athens. The promise of free pizza delivery in thirty minutes was an immediate hit in the small town, and within a few weeks of opening, Domino's there held a near-75 percent market share, reports Leonard in *Living the Faith*.[10] Soon thereafter, Heddle opened another shop in Columbus, near the Ohio State University. Staying in close proximity to college campuses continued to lead to success for Domino's; even as the franchise expanded, 75 percent of the stores were in college towns or around military bases as of 1978. Monaghan knew his customer—primarily young, single males[11]—and continued to set up shop near where they spent the majority of their time—namely, school and home.

Monaghan's focus on setting up locations near college campuses was a solid one, given the demographics of his target customer, but finding desirable real estate proved to be more challenging than he had expected. "My theory was that we wanted to be on the back of a campus, where the dorms usually were, not on the front, where most of the retail shops were. Oftentimes there were no retail stores on the back side, just cornfields. That was the kind of location I would look for, hoping to find a business that wasn't doing much, something I could convert," Monaghan says.[12] That initial difficulty in finding the type of real estate Monaghan was after eventually led the company off that well-defined path and into some new challenges when Domino's "decided to go after the residential market without campus stores as anchors."[13]

"If it doesn't fit with pizza night, it probably doesn't fit on our menu."

—JOE JORDAN,
Domino's Executive Vice President

CHAPTER FOUR

KEEPING THINGS SIMPLE

From the outset, Monaghan was extremely clear about what kind of business Domino's was and what it wasn't. That clarity of purpose helped the business stay on course for decades, by concerning itself with becoming the best at pizza delivery, rather than being the best in other areas. For example, Domino's didn't try to compete on providing the broadest selection of toppings, creating an opulent dining area, or an expansive menu.

No, Domino's Pizza aspired to be the best pizza delivery operation around. Of course, in order to achieve that goal, the company also needed to be strong in other parts of its business. But the organization worked hard not to become distracted by other opportunities along the way. Monaghan's recognition of the importance of specialization in business evolved over time, but was sparked by his early experience culling the list of pizza sizes; he found that fewer options was very good for business.

> From the outset, Monaghan was extremely clear about what kind of business Domino's was and what it wasn't. That clarity of purpose helped the business stay on course for decades, by concerning itself with becoming the best at pizza delivery, rather than being the best in other areas.

A Narrow Menu

Reducing the number of potential pizza sizes customers could order simplified many aspects of the business, from measuring portions to stocking different-sized boxes. Back in 1960, Monaghan saw that cutting out six-inch pizzas and submarine sandwiches from the menu boosted profitability immediately. Part of the problem with the smaller pizzas, he admits in a *New York Times* interview,[1] was that he wasn't charging enough. "The real problem," he remembers, "was that we were selling 6-inch pizzas for 30 cents and free delivery. One night, someone telephoned an order for 12 pizzas, and I said: 'We're not taking any more orders for 6-inch pizzas.' I switched to bigger ones, up to 16 inches, and that night started making money."

Seeing the immediate impact of that decision would shape later decisions, with Monaghan always erring on the side of simplicity and niche focus.

Domino's limited menu existed for decades with just a few offerings. "From its founding until the early 1990s, the menu at Domino's Pizza was kept simple relative to other fast food restaurants, to ensure efficiency of delivery."[2] By not providing sit-down dining, as was typical of nearly all restaurants of the day, Domino's could keep the size of its storefront small—extra small, really, since the operation relied on supplies stocked at the nearby commissary, rather than in a large storeroom—as well as its workforce, since it didn't need hosts or waitstaff either.

According to *Adweek*, "Historically, Domino's menu consisted solely of one style of pizza crust in two sizes (12-inch and 16-inch), 11 toppings, and Coca-Cola as the only soft drink option."[3] It wasn't until 1989 that anything new was added to the menu, in the form of a new pizza crust—deep dish, or pan pizza, in response to research that indicated that 40 percent of pizza buyers preferred a thicker crust.

In contrast, the fast-food leader of 1960 was McDonald's, which was in the process of expanding its menu. At the time, McDonald's had six different beverage choices. In 1965, the Filet-O-Fish was introduced, followed later by the short-lived roast beef sandwich in the late '60s, breakfast options in the mid '70s, chicken nuggets in 1983, then salads, and, in 1991, the floodgates seemed to have opened, with McDonald's introducing several new menu choices. Variety continued to reign from then on, with everything from pasta to lobster to chicken wings, snack wraps, and McFlurries appearing on the menu in the next couple of decades.[4] McDonald's evolved from a burger joint to a veritable buffet of fast-food fixings.

In contrast, it took about thirty years for Domino's to venture beyond pizza. The first non-pizza item added to the Domino's menu was breadsticks, which debuted in 1992.[5] In 1993, there was another addition—an extra-large-size pizza. Called "The Dominator," it consisted of thirty slices.[6]

It wasn't until 2002 that Domino's dared to add any entree that wasn't pizza to its menu. That year, Domino's rolled out chicken designed to be an alternative to chicken wings. Later, other types of pizza were added, including Philly Cheese Steak pizza, followed by Brooklyn Style pizza, which was a crunchy thin crust. In 2008, as Subway was gaining steam, Domino's rolled out four new submarine sandwiches. The next year, pasta was added to the menu, by way of its Bread Bowl Pasta.

Believing that Domino's original pizza flavor had lost its way, the company threw out its old recipe in 2010 and started fresh, building a new original pizza "from the crust up." Shortly thereafter, the deep dish pizza of old was replaced with a new pan pizza. (In 2013, a vegan pizza was also developed by Domino's Israel using a soy-based cheese for the Israeli market only.)[7]

A Focus on Efficiency

In addition to keeping the chain's menu lean and mean, Monaghan was always on the lookout for opportunities to improve the company's production process itself. He is reported to have visited and studied more than three hundred rival pizzerias[8] to identify the best operational techniques. And when he believed he could improve on what other pizza shops were doing, he invented his own processes.

> " In addition to keeping the chain's menu lean and mean, Monaghan was always on the lookout for opportunities to improve the company's production process itself. He is reported to have visited and studied more than three hundred rival pizzerias to identify the best operational techniques.

Thomas Dicke described Monaghan's approach in *Franchising in America*:

Monaghan's own experiences in the shop led to further refinements. Before the end of the first year, he restructured the interior of the store and rearranged counters, coolers, and work areas to improve the flow of work in all phases of the operation from order taking to delivery. When completed, Monaghan's system was reminiscent of those developed by the managers of White Castle Hamburgers in the 1920s, the McDonald brothers in the 1940s, and other fast-food pioneers. In each case, success depended on adapting the techniques of mass production to the restaurant business. In taking this approach, Monaghan, like the others, viewed the production process as a unified whole, requiring the standardization of materials, thoughtful placement of equipment, and detailed division of labor—all geared to achieve continuous production of a limited product line. And as in the case of other fast-food pioneers, Monaghan's marketing strategy of speedy service and uniform quality led him to a mass-production system. He found that during peak times, the only way to ensure fast delivery was to create a comprehensive and coordinated system of production that covered every step in the pizza-making process.[9]

As previously mentioned, he also upgraded cooking equipment as the opportunity arose, or as he came across machines that were superior to what Domino's was using at the time. The purchase of "Big Red," the monster pizza oven, was one example. Dicke, of *Franchising in America,* said:

> Other changes included the installation of a "Ferris wheel" type of revolving oven, which could accommodate more pies in less space than conventional ovens, and the practice of placing pizzas on rigid screens rather than directly on the oven shelves, which allowed for faster, easier handling and reduced the losses from misshaped pies.[10]

Monaghan scouted for better equipment to use at every point in the production process. As mentioned in Reference for Business's profile of Domino's Pizza, Inc.:

> Looking for equipment ideas at a Chicago convention, he found a meat-grinder which he used to chop cheese as well as mix consistent pizza dough in less than a minute, in contrast to standard mixers, which took eight to ten minutes to mix dough. Dough, once mixed, was stored on oiled pans; although covered by towels, the outside edges of the dough hardened. Monaghan discovered an air-tight fiberglass container that stored dough very well, and his practice later became a standard in the industry.[11]

The meat grinder was a step up because Domino's could use it "not only to shred cheese but also mix dough nine times faster than a standard mixer."[12] Finding multifunctional machinery was a win.

But Monaghan also looked for ways to speed the baking process without equipment, including applying toppings. In *Pizza Tiger*, Monaghan said, "During my days as a pizza maker, I perfected a hand motion for cheesing that worked well. I'd roll my hand over, palm down to palm up, like dealing cards. It was quick, easy, accurate, and wasted no cheese."[13] Monaghan concedes, though, that he was not the master cheeser—Terry Voice was. "He had a little flourish in his wrist motion that made the cheese just flow like liquid and spread evenly over the entire pie." Additionally, Monaghan developed a technique for cutting the pizza into slices using a small cutter, which was about two inches in diameter. He thinks the current use of larger three-inch wheels "is slow and inefficient," but observes "the larger wheels came into favor mainly because they keep your knuckles away from the hot surface of the pizza."[14]

He also looked at the back end, at delivery. Tim McIntyre, executive vice president of communications and investor relations, says that the insulated bag used to keep pizzas hot during delivery was a Domino's innovation. To improve the delivery experience for customers, Domino's also reduced its delivery radius for its stores from nine minutes, which was the original geographic area for each store, to six minutes, says McIntyre. It will open new stores to fill that three-minute delivery radius void, he explains.

Centralizing Supply Delivery

Beyond working on economies of motion in the pizza mixing and baking process, Monaghan also centralized much of the preparation process in a single, centrally located commissary. Setting up a commissary reduced the footprint needed at each retail storefront and removed responsibility for prepping all of the ingredients. All the stores needed to do was assemble, bake, and deliver. In 1978, the commissary operation had grown large enough that it needed someone to manage it. Monaghan hired Don Vlcek to head the commissaries, which were then serving 168 Domino's locations,[15] and further improve how they functioned.

The commissaries were an operation of regionalized locations that produced and distributed ingredients and supplies to all the Domino's pizza shops. "Vlcek streamlined the commissaries and would take the best practices of one commissary and apply them to all."[16] For example:

"When he discovered that one commissary saved on laundry bills by rinsing out the towels used to dry trays, making them last a week before cleaning was necessary, Vlcek made all other commissaries do the same. When he found that another commissary's manager was buying from a local cheese distributor instead of a less expensive national one, the manager reworked his purchasing policies. Vlcek moved sauce-mixing from the commissaries to the company's tomato-packing plant, which resulted in highly consistent, quality pizza sauce. Once Vlcek had taken care of the basics, in one eight-month period he opened a new commissary a month, all with state-of-the-art equipment."[17]

As a result, by 1986, eight years after Vlcek took the helm of the commissary operation, it was a "$315 million independent business unit that supplies things like dough, toppings, mechanical equipment, and promotional items for the pizza franchisees. Compound annual growth [since Vlcek started] has been 75 percent. Employment has soared to well over

1,700 people at 27 commissaries across the US, Canada, and West Germany," said Tom Peters on his blog about Domino's back in 1986.[18]

Looking back, Monaghan reflected on the company's success at that time to *Legatus Magazine*:

> You could not be more focused: We had one company—
> Domino's Pizza. It had one type of store—pizza delivery—with
> no sit-down facilities. During our best years (the 1980s) we of-
> fered pizzas in only two sizes and one drink, Coca-Cola. In most
> stores, the hours were short: 4:30 pm-12:30 am. Central stations
> (commissaries) processed all of the food so that the stores could
> stay focused on "handling the rush"—a phrase referring to
> keeping up with the orders during the peak hours. In the 1980s
> we grew from 300 to 5,000 stores. We were the fastest-growing
> restaurant chain in history at that time. Our market share of
> pizzas delivered was 54 percent.[19]

That focus and obsession with continuous improvement is what fueled the company's growth for several decades. But it wasn't until 2019 that Domino's hit the top of the sales charts.

"Our [first] store didn't cater to the sit-down trade. We had only two small tables in the front part, and I don't think more than four customers could sit there comfortably to eat. We had to depend on delivery and carry-outs."

—TOM MONAGHAN

CHAPTER FIVE

FOCUSING ON DELIVERY

"**W**e did not invent delivery, but Domino's was the first pizzeria to focus on it almost entirely," says Tim McIntyre, executive vice president of communications and investor relations for Domino's in an interview for the Pizza Hall of Fame.[1] Recalling the start of the business, he says, "The initial days were slow; it was December, and kids weren't out much. Delivering pizza to the dorms is what helped turn the business around." It was a savvy strategy for increasing sales.

Depending on whom you ask, pizza delivery itself originated somewhere between 1889, when the first pizza was said to have been delivered in Italy to Queen Margherita,[2] and the 1940s in the US. According to *Time* magazine, "By 1944, restaurants in New York City offered pizza that could be 'ordered to take home,' which were 'packed, piping hot, in special boxes for that purpose.' A few years later, Los Angeles would again prove to be on top of the world's delivery needs, when a pizza joint named Casa D'Amore began offering what is thought to be one of the first examples of free delivery."[3]

> Recalling the start of the business, he says, "The initial days were slow; it was December, and kids weren't out much. Delivering pizza to the dorms is what helped turn the business around." It was a savvy strategy for increasing sales.

Not that Domino's had many other options for driving up sales beyond delivery initially. Describing the early days in Domino's history, when there was a single pizzeria, Funding Universe observed: "The store Monaghan bought had little room for sit-down dining; from the start, delivery was key. The first drivers, laid-off factory workers, agreed to work on commission."[4] The only way to sell more pizzas was to physically bring them to buyers, who, until the late 1940s, traveled more by bike and walking than by car.

Delivery as a Competitive Barrier to Entry

Delivery was also a way to gain a competitive advantage, Monaghan thought. Explains McIntyre in a 2019 interview, "The delivery business was so hard that he thought there would be little competition—that delivery would be a barrier to entry to other competitors." At the time, Pizza Hut owned sit-down dining and Little Caesars dominated carryout, so, with Domino's focused on delivery, the three companies could coexist, McIntyre says.[5]

Monaghan explained the delivery focus to *Fortune Small Business* this way:

> Delivery at the time was pretty minimal, so I decided to focus on that, and it was the best thing I've done. Nobody thought you could make money on delivery. Most places just delivered to get some volume before they could afford to cut out the delivery. But I thought I could do it. It was a challenge. I just had to figure out how.[6]

In the 1950s and 1960s, having someone else cook for you often involved eating out at a restaurant. Although about 50 percent of Pizza Hut's business consisted of take-out orders then, it was more focused on bringing customers *into* its restaurants. "In 1963, Pizza Hut designed a building style that was adopted for all restaurants throughout the chain. It had a large dining room with seating for 80 people, and an expanded menu was introduced. The company shifted to a thicker crust pizza and added several different types of pizzas, including Chicago pan-style pizzas."[7] Takeout was gravy, while sit-down dining was Pizza Hut's bread and butter. Delivery might not even have been on its radar at that point.

But authors Gary Allen and Ken Albala explain that the market shifted after the war.

> Modern pizza delivery picked up after World War II, when pizzerias started popping up all over the United States due to the increased use of cars and soldiers' newfound cravings. Domino's Pizza founder Tom Monaghan was the first person

to focus on quality delivery in the 1960s, when no one thought it was profitable.[8]

How Delivery Became King

When Domino's was still DomiNick's, Monaghan was promoting "fast free delivery" as a selling point for his pizza. Then, when he opened his second location, in Mount Pleasant, he distributed thousands of flyers offering free pizza delivery.[9] That location quickly surpassed his original Ypsilanti location in sales. Delivery became Domino's hallmark.

By 1986, Monaghan had so refined his formula that growing the business was nearly just a math equation. Author James Leonard explains in *Living the Faith*:

> They'd pick a spot based on its population, divide it into delivery quadrants, rent or build stores in each quadrant, and then saturate the area with advertising. With a seemingly endless stream of franchisees coming up through the system and TSM Leasing ready to underwrite their startup costs, along with Dave Black's operational expertise, Sam Fine's marketing skills, and Don Vlcek's finely tuned commissaries backing them, Monaghan believed he had a near-perfect, near-limitless moneymaking machine.[10]

As with other parts of its business, Domino's continued to innovate its delivery process, starting with the pizza box itself. Monaghan is actually credited with the first use of corrugated cardboard for pizza boxes, rather than the typical coated paper box that had been used for years. According to The Balance Small Business website, "[Monaghan] invented an insulated box that would not only keep the pizza warm but also support the weight of multiple boxes on top of it, allowing several to be delivered at once, without the box's lid sagging and causing the cheese to be stuck to the top."[11] He worked with Triad Containers in Detroit "to create a cardboard box that could be scored properly for folding while remaining strong enough to hold its form and protect its contents," The Paper and Packaging Board reported. The underlying challenge with pizza boxes is that, due to the cheesy goodness contained within, moisture and oil from the toppings frequently soak the bottom and make its construction weaker, or the cheese sticks to the top of the floppy box, separating it from the pie. But, thanks to its thickness, corrugated cardboard could absorb more oil than a single layer of thick paper and protect the layer of cheese from being squashed.

> As with other parts of its business, Domino's continued to innovate its delivery process, starting with the pizza box itself. Monaghan is actually credited with the first use of corrugated cardboard for pizza boxes, rather than the typical coated paper box that had been used for years.

Serious Eats claims that the box has become a standard for the pizza industry, "right down to the way the box base doubles over itself to lock into the base, known appropriately as 'Michigan style.'"[12] Part of the innovation lies in the fact that the scored cardboard can be stored flat and only constructed as needed, when an order is placed. That saves considerable space.

Even before Monaghan designed the sturdier delivery box, however, Domino's had made a big leap forward with its thermal insulated delivery bag. Domino's actually patented its bag, which was designed to keep pizzas oven-hot from the time they were placed in a cardboard box until handed to the customer at their doorstep. The bag made its first delivery around 1983, according to *PMQ* magazine, though there were several technologies used before it.

> **Domino's actually patented its bag, which was designed to keep pizzas oven-hot from the time they were placed in a cardboard box until handed to the customer at their doorstep. The bag made its first delivery around 1983.**

In the days of old, pizza delivery guys only had a few unconventional ways to deliver hot food. Some wrapped pizza boxes with blankets to keep them hot until they reached their destination. Others used Styrofoam coolers. Oh, don't forget those old, metal Sterno boxes that funked up the car with the smell of burning Sterno fuel. These metal boxes were also cumbersome and a pain in the butt to deal with.[13]

Today, reports *PMQ,* the thermal bag is perhaps the most widely used, "but there are also bags that use heat-retaining disks, internal electric heaters and induction heated bags that use pellets that heat up to warm the bag."

Domino's is also responsible for inventing the now-ubiquitous detachable 3D cartop sign,[14] which alerts customers that their pizza is in the driveway. Now used in a wide variety of industries, such as taxis and driving schools, the 3D sign was an ingenious way of advertising the company in all the neighborhoods that it served, at no incremental cost.

Monaghan had a knack for recognizing an opportunity for improvement and taking action on it. In large part, that's what has helped Domino's gain the upper hand in the pizza market—continuous innovation, which started with its focus on delivery.

"Domino's biggest innovation was delivery, which they successfully sold through the famous promise to deliver your pizza within 30 minutes of ordering, or it was free. This idea only came about after years of finding ways to make the entire process faster."

—*INC.* MAGAZINE

CHAPTER SIX

THE THIRTY-MINUTE GUARANTEE

More than any other feature, Domino's is perhaps best known for its speedy delivery, because that is what Tom Monaghan decided very early on would be the company's primary differentiator. In particular, delivery in thirty minutes or less became Domino's promise almost from the beginning. It had been part of Monaghan's vision for the company dating as far back as the first store, according to a profile in *Entrepreneur* magazine:

> "The idea of stressing 30-minute delivery grew out of my insistence on giving customers a quality pizza," Monaghan explains in *Pizza Tiger*. "It didn't make sense to use only the best ingredients if the pizza was cold and tasteless when the customer got it." To motivate his drivers to make their deliveries as fast as possible, Monaghan gave bonuses to those who collected the most cash.[1]

At the time, pizzerias delivered pizzas when they were ready, whenever that happened to be. There was no standard. Pizzas might arrive in "anywhere from 20 minutes to two hours be-cause no other company thought of controlling the delivery process. From a competitive perspective, customers chose a pizza based on taste and price, not delivery."[2] Monaghan claims that the company's decision to focus on delivery made his first shop on the campus of Eastern Michigan University "the busi-est pizzeria in the country."[3]

Origins of the Thirty-Minute Promise

The first evidence of the thirty-minute delivery promise ap-peared in 1973, when Domino's introduced an offer of "a half hour or a half dollar off."[4] That year was a turning point in the company's history, according to historians at Funding Universe. That promise apparently got the attention of the competition, some of which began to incorporate delivery speed into their brand messaging, and which then ratcheted up the stakes.

It took another ten years, however, before Domino's was will-ing to go all in on thirty-minute deliveries. In 1984, the com-pany began guaranteeing delivery within thirty minutes, or the pizza was free.[5] The pizza was free if it was late until 1986, when the offer shifted to $3 off the order if it arrived after more than thirty minutes. The *New York Times* claimed the delivery offer served "as the backbone of Domino's rapid growth into the largest pizza-delivery company in the country."[6]

" It took another ten years, however, before Domino's was willing to go all in on thirty-minute deliveries. In 1984, the company began guaranteeing delivery within thirty minutes, or the pizza was free. The *New York Times* claimed the delivery offer served "as the backbone of Domino's rapid growth into the largest pizza-delivery company in the country."

The truth is that although timely delivery appeared to be based heavily on the skill or speed of the delivery driver, whether the pizza arrived on time depended more on what happened inside the store than when it left. How quickly orders were taken and processed, how soon the pizza-making was started, and how fast the pizza was placed in the oven had a bigger impact on on-time delivery than travel time, Domino's indicated:[7]

As the anchor leg of the relay team, the delivery person was never charged by the company for late deliveries, said Tim McIntyre, a spokesman for the company, which is based in Ann Arbor, Mich. In fact, any pizza that had not left the store within 25 minutes of the placement of the order was automatically marked "late," he said, and delivered with the appropriate price adjustment.

The Downside of Focusing on Speed

However, the delivery guarantee did create problems for the company. By 1989, more than twenty deaths had occurred involving Domino's drivers, Funding Universe reports, and pressure was mounting on Domino's to help stem the accidents. One franchisee went so far as to hire an off-duty police officer to monitor the driving habits of its delivery drivers to ensure they weren't speeding. By then the outcry had grown too loud to be ignored. Consumer groups against the thirty-minute delivery guarantee had even banded together to form People against Dangerous Delivery to lobby against Domino's practices.

Opposition to the thirty-minute delivery guarantee culminated in a high-profile lawsuit in 1993 involving Domino's and a delivery driver who had run a red light in 1989, hitting another driver and causing her head and spinal cord injuries. That victim, Jean Kinder of St. Louis, won nearly $79 million in damages as a result and caused Domino's to reevaluate the efficacy of its delivery guarantee. Not wanting to continue the impression that its drivers were speeding, or that they were unsafe, Domino's immediately pivoted its promotional offer.

Instead of tying a refund to delivery speed, Domino's turned back to its Total Satisfaction Guarantee as a core message, which promised that if for any reason you were not satisfied with your order, the company would remake the pizza or refund the payment.

The Noid Premieres

When Domino's stopped its "thirty minutes or it's free" promise in 1986, it also debuted a new company mascot, named the

Noid. A play on the word "annoyed," marketing firm Group 243 conceived of the character, which many considered to be "one of the most obnoxious mascots of all time," reported Priceonomics.[8] It was described as:

> A troll-like creature [which was] outfitted in a skin-tight red onesie with rabbit-like ears and buck-teeth. Will Vinton, whose studio animated the creature, described it as a "physical manifestation of all the challenges inherent in getting a pizza delivered in 30 minutes or less." . . . Throughout the late '80s, Domino's ran a series of commercials in which the Noid set about attempting to make life an utter hell for pizza consumers.

Fast Company went even further in its negative assessment of the Noid: "Even compared to the worst corporate mascots, the Noid was a unique grotesquerie. A gibbering, pot-bellied, buck-toothed pervert squeezed into a skintight rabbit costume, the Noid was a Hamburglar-like character wholly devoted to delaying pizza deliveries."[9]

Despite its crazy appearance, the Noid was a big hit with consumers. Domino's advertising messages for the next three years frequently cautioned pizza lovers to "Avoid the Noid," and promised that its pizzas were "Noid-proof." So popular was the red troll that it spawned two separate video games and a line of toys and merchandise. Part of its appeal may have been the fact that Will Vinton Studios, which created the California Raisins, was hired to bring the Noid to life through Claymation. It was weird and cool and crazy all wrapped into one, and consumers couldn't get enough.

Until they did. The Noid campaign was immediately terminated when a mentally disturbed twenty-two-year-old used a .357 Magnum to take two Domino's employees hostage. Kenneth Lamar Noid believed that Domino's had created the character to persecute him, and although the employees escaped unharmed, the damage to the brand had been done. The Noid was pulled from all spots for many years.

> Despite its crazy appearance, the Noid was a big hit with consumers. Domino's advertising messages for the next three years frequently cautioned pizza lovers to "Avoid the Noid," and promised that its pizzas were "Noid-proof." So popular was the red troll that it spawned two separate video games and a line of toys and merchandise.

That misstep, which Domino's could never have foreseen or planned for, did not dampen the company's rise to leading pizza purveyor, however. By 1993, Domino's was the largest pizza-delivery company in the US, according to the *New York Times*.[10] Today, Domino's continues to refine and improve the delivery aspect of its operations while building on its cost-efficient store model and a delivery- and carryout-oriented store design.

"At the age of 61, reflecting on my life and the goals I have yet to fulfill, I have decided to retire from active involvement in Domino's Pizza and devote more time to my charitable endeavors."

—TOM MONAGHAN

CHAPTER SEVEN

MONAGHAN TRIES TO SELL THE BUSINESS, TWICE

Raised a Catholic with early hopes of becoming a priest, Tom Monaghan's faith has always guided his life, including how he ran Domino's. Exploring his faith may have taken a back seat in some respects during the frenetic early days of running the pizza business purely because he barely had time to sleep and eat. But it was never unimportant. Even then, Monaghan was a self-described "practicing Catholic—going to Mass on Sundays and doing the minimal things you had to do to stay in sanctifying grace and keep it there."[1]

In the early 1980s, his faith came back into the forefront, especially as he heard about other business and sports leaders finding time for it. He explained this part of his religious journey in the *National Catholic Register*.

In 1984, I started going to Mass every day after hearing that [former coach of the Miami Dolphins] Don Shula went to Mass

every day. And then not too long after that, one of the sermon-
ettes by [my pastor] Father Robert Lunsford was on how Mary,
in one appearance after another, stressed saying the rosary. That
struck me as something that Mary wants. It must be important
or she wouldn't be going to all that trouble to get the point
across. I figured that the least I could do is spend 15 minutes
saying the rosary every day.[2]

That renewed focus on faith then triggered a number of
other personal decisions that ultimately affected Domino's.
Charitable gifts from The Domino's Foundation rose from
$157,000 to "an expected $2 million" in 1989, the primary re-
cipient that year being a mission in Honduras.[3] From there, the
money spilled into more political issues.

The NOW Boycott

As his personal focus and interests evolved in the late 1980s,
Monaghan began supporting charities and causes that reflected
his Catholic faith. One such donation he made in 1988 was to
help fight a statewide measure to preserve state funding for
abortion services. Monaghan was pro-life and his financial support and that of The Domino's Foundation reflected that. The
New Yorker reported on the donation:

In 1988, Michigan voters were considering a referendum that
would have preserved state funding of abortion, which the state
legislature had voted to end the year before. For pro-choice
forces, it was an early attempt to use the referendum process to
guarantee women's access to abortion.[4]

“ As his personal focus and interests evolved in the late 1980s, Monaghan began supporting charities and causes that reflected his Catholic faith. One such donation he made in 1988 was to help fight a statewide measure to preserve state funding for abortion services. In response, the National Organization for Women (NOW) called for a nationwide boycott of Domino's.

In response, the National Organization for Women (NOW) called for a nationwide boycott of Domino's. The boycott, announced in January 1989, was sparked by Monaghan's decision to cancel a NOW fundraiser in 1988 that was to be held at Domino's Farms, the Domino's corporate headquarters in Ann Arbor. Monaghan rescinded his permission to host the event there after he learned that the fundraiser's proceeds would support People's Campaign for Choice. In 1988, he also donated $110,000 to the Committee to End State-Funded Abortions.

Boycotters claim that Monaghan uses pizza profits to promote irresponsible land development, limit women's reproductive freedom, break unions, and promote a right-wing agenda in Central America.[5]

After nearly a year of the boycott, Monaghan shocked the business community when he announced his intention to sell

Domino's in 1989. When asked if the boycott was the reason, Monaghan denied it, saying:

"The question's been asked if the boycott of Domino's Pizza . . . has affected my thinking," Monaghan wrote recently in a guest column for the *Los Angeles Times* (9/17/89). "It probably hasn't because the boycott really hasn't hurt business. However, I wouldn't want my support of such social issues to hurt my franchisees in the future."[6]

Despite Monaghan's denial, *Detroit News* columnist Bob Talbert reported in his column on October 22, 1989, that "there are currently more sub $5,500-a-week outlets—read unprofitable—than ever before."[7]

Years later, however, Monaghan admitted that the NOW boycott was what prompted his decision to step away from the company he had founded by selling it:

Well, that was about late '88, and more than anything that's what led to trying to sell the company. I felt a boycott like they had started could have an impact on a lot of people whose livelihood depended on Domino's. And I felt I could risk my livelihood, and I was willing to do that, but I didn't have the right to risk that of others. So, I decided to sell the company because if there was something I should do, like the thing I did that got me into that boycott, then I wanted to be able to do it.[8]

In 1989, Domino's had nearly 5,000 pizzerias in the US and just under 260 in other countries.[9] Although Pizza Hut was the top pizza outlet, with 38 percent of the market, Domino's was picking up steam at number 2, controlling 32 percent of the market.[10] According to the *New York Times*, the company employed about 40,000 people worldwide. Sales in 1988 were $2.3 billion, with a net income of $6.1 million. A year later, sales were $2.5 billion and net income was down to $5.1 million.[11]

Monaghan Steps Aside

Even before the NOW boycott put pressure on Domino's operations, the company was already hard at work trimming the fat in an effort to improve profitability. Starting in 1987, according to the *New York Times*, "Domino's Pizza Inc. said it would trim jobs and reduce health benefits in a cost-cutting effort that was accelerated when its founder, Tom Monaghan, said recently that he might sell the pizza delivery company. The company will lay off nearly 100 employees at its Ann Arbor headquarters and 13 offices throughout the country, a spokesman, Ron Hingst, said. Costs of health-care benefits, now paid by the company, will be shared by employees."[12]

Following rumors that he was considering selling, Monaghan followed that up with confirmation in late 1989 that he was, indeed, talking to potential suitors. He would be devoting more time to his philanthropic activities, he said. In a letter to the eight hundred Domino's franchise owners, Monaghan told them, "It is not fair to give divided attention to Domino's Pizza and my foundation work."[13]

William Leach, an analyst with Donaldson, Lufkin & Jenrette, estimated that Domino's would fetch around $1 billion when sold, though Monaghan had put a $1.2 billion price tag on the corporation.[14] Coca-Cola and PepsiCo, owner of Pizza Hut, were said to be bidders. Monaghan named Dave Black, who had twice been the top Domino's Franchisee of the Year,[15] as president and chief operating officer so that Monaghan could move on. Then he attempted to structure a buyout in the form of an employee stock ownership plan, but was unsuccessful. Although no longer involved in the day-to-day management of the company, Monaghan became even more committed to separating himself from the company and some of the trappings of wealth that he had acquired, such as the Detroit Tigers baseball team and several real estate holdings. He continued to hold firm to the $1.2 billion sale price.

But sales had fallen and Domino's had to turn its attention to stopping the bleeding. In the spring of 1990, the company cut its public relations and international marketing departments, as well as its executive management and support staff, to reduce expenses and boost profitability, Funding Universe says. "Payroll that year decreased by $24 million." Those efforts continued in 1991 when the company closed approximately 125 unprofitable locations and wrote off $41 million against earnings. Sales of $2.6 billion in 1990 fell to $1.7 billion in 1991.[16] About half the pizzas Domino's sold in 1991 had been discounted.[17]

Store expansion had also slowed, with Domino's opening fewer than three hundred units in 1989 and 1990 when it had regularly added an average of five hundred stores a year through the 1980s. Owning 98 percent of Domino's stock, Monaghan then announced he would sell a portion of his shares as part of an initial public offering (IPO) planned for 1992, while still retaining majority ownership.[18] He bundled several of his holdings as part of the IPO deal, which, looking back, is probably why that, too, was not successful.

> " But sales had fallen and Domino's had to turn its attention to stopping the bleeding. In the spring of 1990, the company cut its public relations and international marketing departments, as well as its executive management and support staff, to reduce expenses and boost profitability. Store expansion had also slowed, with Domino's opening fewer than three hundred units in 1989 and 1990 when it had regularly added an average of five hundred stores a year through the 1980s.

The public stock offering stalled when Wall Street discovered the price included a collection of nonpizza operations—a holding company, an investment company, and the Ave Maria Foundation among others—that lost between $40 and $70 million a year.[19]

Forced to face that he would be unable to sell Domino's until its financial future turned the corner, Monaghan announced on December 7, 1991, that he was retaking control and returning to Domino's full-time.[20] "I didn't have any choice but to come back," he told *Fortune Small Business*. "We were half-a-billion dollars in debt."[21]

> "Forced to face that he would be unable to sell Domino's until its financial future turned the corner, Monaghan announced on December 7, 1991, that he was retaking control and returning to Domino's full-time. "I didn't have any choice but to come back," he told *Fortune Small Business*. "We were half-a-billion dollars in debt."

Monaghan Returns, Refocuses, and Sells to Bain

On his return, Monaghan immediately got to work in righting Domino's financial ship. He purged the executive team, then did so again later in 1992. He closed four more regional headquarters, and rolled out a new pizza with more cheese and more topping options.[22] Although progress wasn't evident immediately, as sales fell to $2.375 billion in 1993 from a $2.6 billion high in 1990, and the number of stores dropped from 5,428 in 1991 to 5,099,[23] Monaghan kept at the expense cutting. By 1993, "He'd cut everything he could by closing stores, commissaries, and regional offices, and firing 600 administrative employees and executives."[24] Then things started to turn around.

Year-end 1994 sales figures were up at Domino's for the first time in five years, to $2.5 billion. That upward swing continued for five more years under Monaghan's leadership, into 1998.[25] That was the year that Monaghan sold a controlling 93 percent stake in Domino's to Bain Capital, Inc., which renamed it Domino's, Inc. officially. TheStreet reported that Bain had purchased 6,100 Domino's stores for $1.1 billion.[26] That same year—1998—Domino's had sales estimated at $3.2 billion, from 4,489 domestic and 1,730 international stores.[27] With Monaghan's retirement, he left Domino's on strong footing and sales on a positive trajectory under Bain's new guidance.

"To be sure, the delivery trend that has quickly spread throughout the restaurant industry is taking hold in many other sectors. . . . And of course, pizza players such as Domino's, Pizza Hut and Papa John's are also facing questions about the potential impact of so much delivery on their core businesses."

—*RESTAURANT BUSINESS*

CHAPTER EIGHT

HOW THE COPYCATS CAUGHT UP

I n the late 1980s, when Monaghan still owned Domino's, pizza had become America's fastest-growing fast food, according to *New York* magazine.[1] During the mid-1980s and early 1990s, the pizza market grew at the fastest rate of any major segment in the restaurant industry.[2] According to a Gallup Poll, "Pizza was the most popular takeout item among the young and single," as of 1987, with deliveries accounting for about 25 per cent of the $8 billion pizza business, reported the *New York Times*, and which was expected to rise to more than 33 percent of the projected $12 billion market by 1990.[3]

It was an appetizing market, with time-starved young professionals fueling the growth. "Feeding the home-delivery trend, analysts say, are dual-income couples, many of whom are starting families. They have enough money to eat out but often not the time or inclination. According to the Bureau of Labor Statistics, both spouses work in 56 percent of American families, and more than one-third of such households earn more than

$50,000 a year."[4] And home delivery, while considered a small portion of the market, was growing "almost twice as fast as take-out or drive-through," the *New York Times* reported. At that point, frozen pizza represented 10 percent of the total pizza market, said *Pizza Today*.

Where convenience was driving delivery of pizzas to consumers, profitability was attracting the business-minded. There was money to be made. "Pizza also packs the greatest profits, with pre-tax margins of 30 percent, compared with average fast-food profits of 9 percent, according to the National Restaurant Association."[5]

By 1992, the *New York Daily News* claimed:

> The pizza industry—both sit-down and off-premises—is a $17 billion business, with off-premises dining driving much of its sales. Since 1987, delivery and carryout together have grown from 65 percent of the industry to 67 percent, or $11.4 billion, according to NPD Crest, a market research firm in Park Ridge, Ill.[6]

With all of the good news coming out about rising opportunities in the pizza business, it's not surprising that Pizza Hut shifted its attention to home delivery. Higher profits, expanding market, and increasing demand were all good reasons on their own, but together they suggested a potential perfect storm that could yield higher sales.

Pizza Hut Muscles into Delivery

The top pizza brand in the 1980s was Pizza Hut, which had owned the sit-down pizza space for decades; Pizza Hut had five thousand storefronts in 1986 to Domino's three thousand a year earlier. But in 1986, it began offering customers a delivery option alongside Domino's. According to the *New York Times* that year:

> After ignoring that part of the market for years, Pizza Hut and others have watched as Domino's helped turn home delivery into the fastest-growing sector in fast food. Capitalizing on the proliferation of two-income households with enough money to eat out, but sometimes not the time or inclination, Domino's aggressive delivery and takeout operation reported sales of $1.08 billion last year. Only Pizza Hut, with $2.15 billion in restaurant sales, is bigger.[7]

Using its considerable financial resources, Pizza Hut invested $75 million in building up a home delivery process and backing it with a promotional punch. Of that $75 million, $50 million was spent on establishing a separate network of "hundreds of specially designed delivery stores," of which Pizza Hut planned on opening four hundred in 1986.[8] Within a year, the *Los Angeles Times* reported, "Pizza Hut, its only nationwide rival in home delivery, has opened 1,000 delivery outlets."[9]

That investment in its delivery operation started to pay off for Pizza Hut almost immediately. In 1988, Pizza Hut reported that home delivery then accounted for approximately 25 percent of its sales and was the fastest-growing segment of its business.[10] By 1991, just three years later, Pizza Hut's delivery sales hit $1 billion.[11]

Before Pizza Hut entered the delivery market in 1986, Domino's virtually dominated that nationwide segment. But between 1989 and 1992, where Pizza Hut watched its share of delivery rise to 19.8 percent in traffic and 20.2 percent in dollars, Domino's saw its share of traffic fall to 46 percent and its share of dollars drop to 46.6 percent.[12] The delivery war was on.

> " That investment in its delivery operation started to pay off for Pizza Hut almost immediately. In 1988, Pizza Hut reported that home delivery then accounted for approximately 25 percent of its sales and was the fastest-growing segment of its business. By 1991, just three years later, Pizza Hut's delivery sales hit $1 billion.

Little Caesars Grabs the Value Niche

Where Pizza Hut had decided to compete with Domino's on delivery, Little Caesars was staking its claim to carryout. Interestingly, where Monaghan established Domino's in Michigan, in 1960, Little Caesars began with a first store, also in Michigan, in Garden City, outside Detroit, in1959. "It offered carryout food only—unusual at the time," reported the *Los Angeles Times*.[13]

In 1962, the first Little Casesars franchise opened in Warren, Michigan, and just seven years later, in 1969, it had opened its fiftieth storefront. Although some locations had offered delivery, by 1971, Little Caesars had seen its future, and its future was carryout-only, Funding Universe[14] says. Like Domino's and Pizza Hut, Little Caesars enjoyed rapid growth through the 1970s and '80s as pizza took hold as a meal favorite. In 1979, Little Caesars introduced a new offer of two pizzas for the price of one, coining the phrase, "Pizza! Pizza!" By 1980, it had 226 units and sales of $63.6 million system-wide. Growth continued unabated, and by the mid-1980s, sales had hit $340 million. Funding Universe summarized Little Caesars positioning as:

> The company achieved successful expansion through an emphasis on several simple concepts: market saturation, two pizzas for the price of one, and carryout only. Approximately 98 percent of Little Caesar units were 1,200- to 1,800-square-foot units offering takeout only—overhead and maintenance on these shops was considerably lower than that of competitors who offered sit-down or even delivery-only service, because the restaurants did not require waiters, waitresses, busboys, dishwashers, or delivery personnel.

Growth ramped up from there, and by 1992, Little Caesars had more than four thousand locations.[15] Depending on whom you talk to, that year or the next, 1993, Little Caesars was said to have overtaken Domino's to become the second-largest pizza chain in America, with $2.1 billion in annual sales.[16]

> **" Depending on whom you talk to, that year or the next, 1993, Little Caesars was said to have overtaken Domino's to become the second-largest pizza chain in America, with $2.1 billion in annual sales.**

More than the other pizza market leaders of the day, Little Caesars positioned itself as the value leader to consumers. "Although all touted value, Little Caesars was far and away the value leader," Encyclopedia.com reported. "Pizza Hut's mainstay was its sit-down, red-roofed restaurants, and Domino's was better known for its delivery service. Pizza Hut and Little Caesars had also stepped up delivery (although Little Caesars originally delivered pizzas in the 1960s, it went to carryout only in the 1970s), but neither could top Domino's in this market segment. Little Caesars had some dine-in outlets, including 'pizza stations' inside Kmart stores, but Pizza Hut ruled the sit-down segment with over 8,600 restaurants."[17] Ultimately, Little Caesars proved not much of a competitor in the pizza delivery space.

Papa John's: The Upstart Chain

Many years after Domino's start, in 1984, John Schnatter "bought $1,600 worth of used restaurant equipment, set it up in a broom closet in the back of his father's tavern and started making pizza."[18] He sold pizzas like hotcakes, and just two years later, started franchising the concept. In 1989, Schnatter moved the company's headquarters from southern Indiana to Louisville, Kentucky.

By 1992, Papa John's Pizza was generating revenues of close to $50 million, Funding Universe[19] reports, and in 1993, Schnatter went public with 232 stores. A year later, Papa John's was the seventh-ranked pizza chain in the US. It took only two more years to hit the number four spot on that same list, according to Encyclopedia.com.[20] Sales at Papa John's continued to ramp up at an impressive rate. "Papa John's (1997 sales: $868 million) is the only one of the four largest pizza chains whose slice of the pie has grown at double-digit rates over the past five years," *Time* reported.[21]

In 1999, Papa John's slid into the third-place spot of top pizza enterprises. He did it by differentiating based on quality *and* delivery. Per *Entrepreneur*, "Schnatter noticed that while national franchises would deliver a pie to your door, the local, individually-owned shops, which made a higher quality product, did not provide the same delivery service. Noticing that gap in the market gave Schnatter the base for his Papa John's business plan: He would make quality pizza and deliver it."[22]

Schnatter explained his thought process to *Business Insider*:

> "At the time, Domino's owned speed, Caesars owned price, Pizza Hut variety, and 65 percent of the marketplace was independents," he said. "So I said, 'What if you had a chain that acted like an independent? What if you had a chain focused on quality?' It's pretty obvious."[23]

Schnatter was also single-minded. Unlike other restaurateurs who got sidetracked by the potential revenue to be earned by adding complementary menu items, like chicken wings or salads or desserts, he stayed "focused on developing the 'Perfect Pizza'" and delivering it to customers in a timely fashion.[24] And, much like Monaghan, Schnatter recognized how much more efficient a commissary system was for sourcing and delivering ingredients. His commissary system "was frequently cited by industry analysts and company officials as a key factor in the success of Papa John's."[25]

But what gave Papa John's a leg up early on was Schnatter's pure commitment to the ideal of the perfect pizza. *Time* magazine[26] wrote about it in 1998:

> Schnatter, 36, who gets visibly excited when talking about the sugar-acid ratio in his pizza, which gives Papa John's pies a distinctively sweet flavor, puts simplicity above all else. Pizza Hut offers more variety; Domino's stresses fast delivery; and

Little Caesars sells the least expensive pies. Papa John's has no seating, offers just two types of pizza—no salads, sandwiches or buffalo wings—and remakes any pies that rate less than an 8 on the company's 10-point scale. If the cheese shows a single air bubble or the crust is not golden brown, to give just two examples, out the offender goes. This obsessive attention to detail has helped earn Papa John's the title of best US pizza chain in surveys conducted by *Restaurants and Institutions* magazine for the past two years.

In the end, despite competition on all sides, by 2019, Domino's had achieved its goal of being the top pizza operation in the country. Granted, it did that not just by a laser focus on delivery, though it certainly did have that. But through the years, it completely overhauled its pizza recipe in an effort to more closely achieve a pizza taste that the majority of Americans would deem the best. It also worked hard to reduce expenses and increase sales, for better profit margins. It enhanced its customer ordering and delivery processing, adding in functionality and communication tools to satisfy customers' hunger for details on when, exactly, their pizza would arrive. Together, those factors put Domino's at the top of the competitive heap.

"Domino's now faces tougher competition from a resurgent Pizza Hut. The Yum! Brands (YUM) owned chain has benefited from its sponsorship deal with the National Football League. . . . Even Papa John's has made a comeback."

—CNN BUSINESS

CHAPTER NINE

COMPETITION HEATS UP

Countless new pizza chains entered the market in the 1980s in response to rising demand for the dish, expanding the worldwide pizza market to multibillion-dollar levels. By 1990, however, market expansion appeared to have peaked. Observers began warning of a slowdown.

In 1991, Gerry Durnell, publisher of *Pizza Today* magazine, told the *Los Angeles Times* that "the market is nearly saturated. As a result, the pizza restaurant business is very competitive."[1] Between 1988 and 1991, he stated, "the number of new pizza restaurants has far exceeded demand" and added that he anticipated an industry shakeout was coming.

The Pizza Market Cools

By the mid-1990s, Pizza Hut, Little Caesars, and Domino's accounted for nearly 50 percent of industry sales, reported the

Los Angeles Times. "Until recently, their shares were neatly divvied up, with industry leader Pizza Hut dominating the sit-down segment, Little Caesar's the carryout niche, and Domino's the delivery area."[2] They were "the Big Three."

> While pizza sales had grown at an annual rate of 10 percent during the 1980s, the National Restaurant Association predicted that pizza would overtake hamburgers as "the nation's top fast food" by 1995.

They were also heading into a "slump." While pizza sales had grown at an annual rate of 10 percent during the 1980s, the National Restaurant Association predicted that pizza would overtake hamburgers as "the nation's top fast food" by 1995.[3] Concerned by that prediction, hamburger joints and fast-food outlets began promoting money-saving deals to stem the tide. The result was slowing pizza demand. Technomic Inc., Chicago restaurant consultants, reported that pizza sales were up only 2.2 percent in 1994—far below the 10 percent increases pizza stores were used to.[4] If they couldn't get growth from consumers, they'd have to take it from one another, the major players seem to have decided all at once.

Pizza seller attention then turned to competing on delivery. In 1995, Pizza Hut and Domino's were reported to each have approximately 35 percent of the delivery market, with independent shops sharing the remaining 30 percent.[5] That's when Little Caesars decided it was time to get in on the pizza delivery action, announcing in 1995 that delivery was already available at 85 percent of its 4,600 outlets. Only a year before, only 155 Little Caesars stores offered delivery.[6]

The Ad Wars Begin

As the market for pizza cooled, competitors also amped up their marketing messages. One of the most aggressive attacks involved Pizza Hut going after Domino's delivery business.[7] In one video from 1991, Pizza Hut touts its delivery service, showing a customer covering up Domino's delivery number with a slip of paper with Pizza Hut's phone number. Other ads promoted the availability of delivery from Pizza Hut, as well as separate ads inviting customers to "Hit the Hut" for dinner.

> Though the leader in total pizza sales, Pizza Hut was second to Domino's in the delivery business and was eager to change that, especially as the market for pizza overall was down. Pizza Hut's strategy "strikes right at the heart of Domino's competitive position," said Nancy Kruse, a principal in Technomic Inc., a Chicago-based fast-food consulting company. Pizza Hut "hits a real hot button with consumers," she added, "whose attitude toward home delivery is, 'I want it when I want it.'"[8]

Though most of Pizza Hut's ads in 1991 were directed squarely at Domino's, by the end of the year, the company switched its message up to focus more on the positives that Pizza Hut offered—its taste, ad execs explained. For the next several months, it tried primarily to take delivery customers away from its competitors.

Over the next few years, industry infighting became the norm, as competitors tried to one-up one another on various pizza fronts. Papa John's was next in the Pizza Wars, with its first national television advertisement picking "a fight with market leader Pizza Hut about whose pizzas are fresher. Irate Pizza Hut executives responded with a federal court lawsuit alleging fraudulent and deceptive advertising."[9]

Then Domino's joined the fray alongside its rival to protest a Papa John's ad. "Domino's and Pizza Hut both have petitioned the National Advertising Division of the Council of Better Business Bureaus to determine whether Papa John's should amend its ads. The chains argued unsuccessfully that Papa John's was pitching its pies as fresher—while implying that competitors used days-old dough and canned tomatoes."[10] They both lost that round.

But Papa John's strategy of emphasizing the taste of its pizzas appeared to strike a nerve and sparked a shift that the majority of pizza competitors then made with their advertising approach. Papa John's suggested its pizzas tasted better than Pizza Hut's or Domino's, so both rivals went on the offensive. Pizza Hut "launched a counterattack—the details of which are secret—called Stopa the Papa."[11] Similarly, Domino's moved away from emphasizing the efficiency of its delivery process and created a new advertising campaign emphasizing the quality of its product.

The Price Wars Commence

As pizza sales slowed, the other strategy pizza chains employed to boost sales was cutting prices, or developing value-oriented products or offerings. A *Los Angeles Times* article explained the move:

> New value-priced products from the two biggest pizza chains—Pizza Hut and Domino's—will escalate the war for market share among fast-food chains. Pizza chains are following the successful lead of the hamburger chains, which used combo and two-for-one deals in 1992 to post greater growth in nationwide customer traffic than the pizza segment did, for the first time in years.[12]

Leading the value charge was Little Caesars, which was the first pizza chain to establish a "value niche" with its two-for-one deal. "In recent years, Pizza Hut and Domino's have responded with deep discounting of premium varieties," reported the *Los Angeles Times*. Pressure from fast-food hamburger joints, like McDonald's, which introduced meal bundles, was also driving a new emphasis on more food for less money.

Pizza Hut came out swinging, with a "Bigfoot" pizza, which was a one-by-two-foot pizza with twenty-one slices ranging in price from $9 to $11. The company's marketing chief predicted that offer alone would generate $1 billion in revenue by 1995, or 23 percent of the chain's total revenue. In response, Domino's began working on its own mega offer, which it named "The Dominator." At thirty slices at the same $9 to $11 price point, Domino's had planned to launch it in July 1993 but ended up announcing it early, in May, under pressure to keep pace with its competitors.[13]

The Dominator was also Domino's first entrée into the carryout business. But perhaps due to its size and rectangular shape, this was the first product Domino's wouldn't deliver—

you had to come pick it up yourself. "Domino's has said it doesn't want to deliver the Dominator out of fear that it would cannibalize sales from the chain's pricier pizzas."[14]

Non-Pizza Competition

The market shifted in the 1990s away from standard pizza, which seemed to be ubiquitous. After the entrance of niche pizza shops, like California Pizza Kitchen, or independent wood-fired pizza businesses, customers could also pick up a pizza at Boston Market or in the frozen food aisle of their grocery store, where some pizzerias had private-labeled a frozen offering. Pizza was everywhere, and at that point, many consumers decided they wanted something more. The new hot market in the 2000s? Fast casual, explained the *Washington Post*:

> The market for fast casual food, which is almost but not quite fast food (I'll get to that in a second), has grown by 550 percent since 1999, more than ten times the growth seen in the fast food industry over the same period, according to data from market research firm Euromonitor. Chipotle, likely the best known purveyor of the category, has seen its sales more than quadruple during that time; Panera, another oft-used example, has watched its sales more than triple; and Shake Shack, the hamburger joint du jour, has done so well that it just went public despite operating only 36 outlets.[15]

Americans still loved pizza, but some nights they wanted a salad, or sushi, or a sub sandwich, among other options. As Chipotle caught on, there was a renewed interest in fresh ingredients across the board. Whatever the dish, customers wanted something that hadn't been frozen. That new preference circled back to impact pizza by 2011. That year, Pizza Marketplace reported that "top-your-own pizza" chains, like MOD and Pieology, were battling to be the industry darling.[16] Despite new pizza company entrants, few ads were shown that were as divisive or aggressive as those seen during the pizza downturn of the 1990s. That was the height of the pizza wars.

"The saga of the prank Domino's video could be a case study of how fast-moving social media can both giveth and taketh away."

—SFGATE

CHAPTER TEN

THE DAMAGING VIDEO PRANK

Although competition continued to ramp up in the 1990s and early 2000s, Domino's held on firmly to its place in the top three national pizza chains, which also consisted of Pizza Hut and Little Casesars. Upstart Papa John's had made solid progress but has long held the fourth spot. Sales of pizza remained steady into the 2000s but were hit hard by the recession that began around 2007 and continued into 2009. Then, just as the economy was picking up steam, Domino's suddenly had to cope with a unique crisis that came out of the blue.

Tough Times

In 2009, the Domino's pizza chain was nearly fifty years old and consisted of 8,700 stores in sixty countries around the world.[1] The company made more than one million deliveries a day and employed more than one hundred thousand people worldwide.[2]

But times were tough in the pizza industry overall, as the US economy was just starting to pull out of the Great Recession, as the last two years had been dubbed. Domino's was already smarting, as were most other businesses, from lower sales across the board. A *Wall Street Journal* article reported:

US franchised same-store sales at Domino's fell 1.7 percent in 2007 and 5.6 percent in the first nine months of 2008. Papa John's is predicting its same-store sales will be flat to down 2 percent this year, and Pizza Hut, whose same-store sales slipped 1 percent in the fourth quarter of 2008, is off to a slower start than expected this year, according to Yum, which has called the division its biggest challenge.[3]

Although US fast-food sales had annual compound growth of 6.4 percent from 2002 to 2007, pizza sales had definitely slowed, rising just 2.5 percent in that same period, according to restaurant consulting firm Technomic, Inc. And when the price of cheese, which accounts for as much as 40 percent of a pizza's cost, rose 42 percent in 2007,[4] on top of cost increases in wheat, meats, tomatoes, cardboard, and energy, according to Domino's, pizzerias cut costs in other areas—namely, marketing and promotions. That was a risky move, since Citigroup Global Markets reports that "85 percent of pizza-chain sales are tied to promotions and discounts."[5] But what really caught Domino's off-guard had nothing to do with rising costs or slim margins; it was an Easter Day prank in 2009.

Crisis Timeline

Easter Sunday, 2009, two bored employees at a Domino's store decided around 5 p.m. it would be funny to film themselves doing unsanitary and disgusting things to pizza ingredients before placing them on pizzas supposedly being prepared for customers. In a total of five videos,[6] a uniformed employee violated several health codes with his actions, including putting cheese up his nose and then placing it on a pizza and sneezing on a sandwich, among other gross moves.

The next day, Monday, April 13, one of the employees uploaded the prank videos—the duo claimed the food was never actually delivered to customers—to YouTube. Within minutes, Domino's began receiving reports that there were videos that were damaging to the brand.

Some sources report *The Consumerist*, a consumer affairs blog, had reposted the videos and also alerted Domino's to their existence,[7] while the *San Francisco Chronicle* claims that the founder of GoodAsYouAre.org, an LGBTQ activist site in New York, was the first to warn Domino's when the videos were posted on that site.[8] The lag time between the videos appearing online and Domino's leadership hearing about it was about thirty to forty-five minutes.

Domino's immediately contacted YouTube and asked that the videos be taken down. According to the *Wall Street Journal*, YouTube responded that it needed a signed statement from the copyright holder—namely, the person who uploaded the video—approving the request.[9]

The challenge then became identifying the employees. Domino's took screenshots of the two individuals in the videos and asked for help from YouTubers and bloggers in locating the Domino's store and the employees responsible for the videos. It didn't take long—around three hours, by some estimates. The *San Francisco Chronicle* reported:

> According to *Ad Age* magazine, Georgetown University student Amy Wilson and her boyfriend Jonathan Drake saw that a Jack in the Box sign was briefly visible in one clip. They used Google satellite images to find locations where a Domino's was near a Jack in the Box.
>
> Meanwhile, Paris Miller, a computer consultant from Northern Kentucky, used information from the video post to trace [one of the accused's] friends to Conover, NC, where there is a Domino's across the street from a Jack in the Box. About three hours after McIntyre received that news, another e-mail came—from Kristy Hammonds, the woman who shot and posted the video.[10]

"I am soo sorry!" Hammonds told McIntyre. "It was fake and I wish everyone knew that."

The good news was that, once it knew which store had been the backdrop for the videos, Domino's could confirm that there had been no orders placed by customers during the time frame when the videos had been recorded.[11]

The company's first priority had been identifying the culprits, contacting any customers who had received tainted food (there had been none), and working with the police to file charges against the two employees and notify the health department.[12] On Tuesday, Domino's officially fired Hammonds, the videographer, and Michael Setzer, the video star.[13] And it communicated back through the company and with *The Consumerist* to the audience that had originally reported the existence of the videos that the culprits had been found.

However, that wasn't the end of the saga. By the end of Tuesday, more than 250,000 people had watched the YouTube videos and were becoming increasingly alarmed. Domino's social media team saw Twitter chat about the videos rising. Users wanted to know whether Domino's knew about the videos. Were the employees caught? Were they for real? What were they doing about it? Customers wanted to know what was happening, and at that particular moment, Domino's was staying mum.

Domino's explained its rationale for not speaking publicly in a *San Francisco Chronicle* article:

"The idea that we were trying to ignore it was false, but do you really need to put out a candle with a fire hose?" McIntyre said. Officials instead used their private Twitter accounts and other social media tactics to answer some of the chatter about the incident and eventually activated a Domino's Twitter account two weeks earlier than planned.[14]

The challenge was that Domino's social media team had only been created about a month before, with plans to establish a new social media presence for the company. They had planned to introduce Domino's to Facebook, Twitter, and other sites about a week after the incident occurred,[15] and now they had to spring into reactive mode, instead of being proactive, as they had initially planned.

By midday Wednesday, YouTube views had hit one million. The first twelve results on Google for "Domino's" included five references to the video.[16] There were even more Twitter discussions happening on the platform about the videos.

Later that afternoon, Domino's had its president, Patrick Doyle, record a two-minute video that was shared on YouTube addressing all the questions and apologizing to its customers. In it, he assured customers that the store where the video was recorded had been completely sanitized and that Domino's would be reviewing its hiring practices.

By Wednesday night, YouTube had removed the original videos after hearing from Hammonds. Domino's continued to communicate with its customers through YouTube, Twitter, and other websites to reassure them the situation had been dealt with.

Post-Crisis

Fortunately, after the first week, online chatter about Domino's fell back to normal levels, but the damage to the company's reputation would last far longer. Per the *Wall Street Journal*:

> Already, a new national study conducted by HCD Research using its Media Curves Web site found 65 percent of respondents who would previously visit or order Domino's Pizza were less likely to do so after viewing the offending video.[17]

The original videos (later removed by YouTube) had been viewed approximately two million times within three weeks, while the Domino's response video had been seen 650,000 times.[18] The *Charlotte Observer* reported that the North Carolina store was closed in September 2009 and the two former employees were charged with felony adulterating of food. One pled guilty to a lesser charge and the other pled no contest.[19]

> " The original videos (later removed by YouTube) had been viewed approximately two million times within three weeks, while the Domino's response video had been seen 650,000 times. In time, the videos became part of Domino's history, and the company was heralded as an example of how to handle a public relations crisis effectively by working quickly to correct the situation and keep in regular contact with its customers.

In time, the videos became part of Domino's history, and the company was heralded as an example of how to handle a public relations crisis effectively by working quickly to correct the situation and keep in regular contact with its customers.

"Brandon's smartest move at Domino's was approving a completely new core recipe for the chain's pizza. . . . It helped redefine how customers view the Domino's brand and led to an influx of new business that has not trailed off."

CHAPTER ELEVEN

A NEW ERA

After successfully managing the video prank on Easter Sunday in 2009, Domino's again faced upheaval later that year when its CEO, David Brandon, announced he was leaving the company right in the middle of relaunching its new pizza. His timing could have been better. However, by the time he stepped down, all the hard work had been done on the new pizza recipe.

Brandon had begun his tenure at Domino's in 1999 and began his departure in 2009 to become athletic director at the University of Michigan, of which he was an alum.

David Brandon's Tenure at Domino's

David Brandon's first contact with Domino's Pizza was in 1969, when he asked his college roommate if he'd like to go grab a slice of pizza. As the story goes, the roommate smiled, told him they didn't have to go anywhere, and then picked up the phone and placed an order for pizza delivery from Domino's.[1] Brandon was then a football player at the University of Michigan, down the road from one of Tom Monaghan's earliest shops.

After Michigan, he was recruited by Procter & Gamble (P&G) thanks to a strong recommendation by head football coach Bo Schembechler. He stayed at P&G five years and then moved on to take a position with Valassis Communications, where he rose to the position of CEO. When he left Valassis after twenty years to take the helm at Domino's, he had no pizza industry experience.

In 1999, Domino's had sales of $3.3 billion, more than 6,200 domestic and international stores, and while delivery was still its core competency, 90 percent of its orders were taken by phone.[2] One of the company's challenges at the time had to do with its human resources. Domino's store-level employee turnover was 158 percent, or 60 percent higher than the restaurant industry's average, reported Pizza Marketplace.[3] Every time a store-level employee left, it cost Domino's $2,500 to replace them. Replacing a store manager cost on the order of $20,000.[4] The *Wall Street Journal* reported:

> [Brandon's] first day at Domino's, he asked about the company's turnover rate. He was told it was 158 percent. "Honest to God, I almost fainted," he says.
>
> After doing some math, he realized Domino's was recruiting, hiring and training 180,000 people a year at the time, including those at franchise stores.

Brandon knew his success would depend in large part on changing the revolving door culture that existed at that time within Domino's. Part of the problem may have been the lack of any kind of formal college recruiting process or employee training or bonus system, according to the *Detroit News*.

Focusing on People

Recognizing the importance of learning the business and shoring up its hiring and retention process, "Brandon put himself through the Domino's store employee training program, and then hit the road to visit hundreds of pizza stores in that first year. His mission, he said, was to open communication between him and operators, so he gave them his personal e-mail address and phone number," Pizza Marketplace[5] reported.

He then relaxed the dress code, introduced a new college recruiting system, developed a way of rewarding employees based on the company's financial success, and launched a comprehensive training program, consisting of classroom and in-store instruction, for new and existing workers. To that end, he had designed and built a working replica of a Domino's store within the company's headquarters to aid in its training process, according to the *Detroit News*.

To underscore his commitment to reducing employee turnover, and providing more support for its workers, Brandon renamed the human resources department "PeopleFirst."[6] But he also invested in tactics to weed out lower performers. "He implemented drug testing for delivery drivers, new financial software to prevent 'shrinkage' and theft, and a ban to prevent hiring former employees who had been fired."[7] With employee recruitment, training, retention, and compensation efforts more in alignment with corporate goals, Brandon turned his attention to expanding the company's product offerings. Meaning, he wanted to ramp up its new product introductions.

New Product Additions

He immediately began making changes, leveraging his consumer products and marketing expertise. Within two years, he had added 758 new Domino's stores and several new non-pizza products—virtually unheard of at Domino's.[8]

> **He immediately began making changes, leveraging his consumer products and marketing expertise. Within two years, he had added 758 new Domino's stores and several new non-pizza products—virtually unheard of at Domino's.**

He started with add-on products—Cheesy Bread and Cinnamon Bread Twists (the first-ever dessert offering)—which were new iterations of existing raw materials, namely pizza dough and toppings. In 2001, sales grew 6.8 percent over the prior year, due in no small part to the additions. So, in 2002, Domino's broke out of its pizza mold and added a chicken menu item—Domino's Pizza Buffalo Chicken Kickers—creating a new product category that would become an important revenue generator.

In 2003, Domino's added other options, including Domino's Dots desserts and the Philly Cheese Steak pizza. The choice of cheese steak was an effort to bring in another American comfort food, said then–vice president of marketing Ken Calwell.

Domino's Dots were "balls of dough baked in cinnamon and sugar and served with a vanilla icing glaze," the company promised. Together, these two new entries helped Domino's grab a little more market share from its formidable competitors.

The following year, in 2004, salads became available in a limited number of Domino's stores.[9] It wasn't until 2016 that salads became a staple in all of its stores, however. But perhaps trying to balance out appealing to the healthy eating crowd and the comfort food lovers, in 2005, Domino's launched the American Classic Cheeseburger Pizza alongside a conjunction with *The Apprentice* TV show.

Brownie Squares were one of the new additions in 2006, which were bite-sized brownie treats accompanied by fudge dipping sauce. The other was a Brooklyn Style Pizza, which was baked with a thinner crust coated in cornmeal for crispiness, and larger slices that could be folded while eaten, like traditional New Yorkers do.

Another dessert was added to the menu in 2007—Oreo Dessert Pizza. While this was not the first dessert menu item, it was one of the first product partnerships and the first positioning of pizza as a dish served as anything but an entrée. The following year, it launched a line of oven-baked sandwiches. That sandwich launch made Domino's the largest sandwich delivery company, essentially overnight. Domino's also debuted the 444 Deal—a value meal consisting of three 10-inch, one-topping pizzas for $4 each.[10]

Most importantly, 2008 was the year that Brandon and head of US operations Patrick Doyle decided to reformulate the original Domino's pizza recipe.[11] In 2009, Domino's "scrapped its 49-year-old pizza recipe and launched its 'new and inspired pizza,'" the company reports.

Improved Store Portfolio

While building a system to attract and reward top workers, and expanding Domino's product line, Brandon was also working to improve the company's overall financial performance. Just a year after taking the helm, Brandon began work on its distribution channel—meaning, its stores. He started by analyzing store performance and then closed or sold to franchisees 146 unprofitable locations. Some stores he relocated to more visible spots. And then he ramped up new store openings.[12] After cutting one hundred administrative positions at the corporate headquarters, he created new roles for product development pros and brand managers—a sign of the company's focus going forward.

He then promoted J. Patrick Doyle, the former senior vice president of US marketing, to run Domino's Pizza International, including opening the two thousandth location outside the US in 2000. The following year, Doyle's division purchased a majority interest in a Netherlands franchisee operating fifty-two Domino's pizza shops in that country. That business then became Domino's regional European office.

By 2002, in just three years, Domino's had increased its store count by nine hundred under Brandon's leadership. That was a feat, given that when Brandon took over, Domino's had lost significant market share to Papa John's and was no longer the top pizza delivery enterprise in the US. But he turned it around.

Brandon focused much of his attention on Domino's US store portfolio, and by 2003, according to Company Histories, 90 percent of its domestic outlets had either been relocated or renovated. Internationally, Domino's exited money-losing markets where necessary, and reallocated its marketing budget to promote its best-performing markets—Canada, Mexico, the UK, Australia, Japan, France, and Brazil. At the start of 2004,

Domino's had 7,300 Domino's locations worldwide and had set its sights on hitting ten thousand, plus one thousand in the US. In 2006, the company celebrated the opening of its eight thousandth store.

> **By 2002, in just three years, Domino's had increased its store count by nine hundred under Brandon's leadership. That was a feat, given that when Brandon took over, Domino's had lost significant market share to Papa John's and was no longer the top pizza delivery enterprise in the US.**

Improvements during Brandon's Tenure

During Brandon's ten years at Domino's, he hit many milestones and chartered a clear course for the company. In all, Domino's store count grew by more than 2,600 locations worldwide. The company's market value doubled, to more than $2 billion, and it went public in 2004.

In 2007, Domino's was among the first pizza ventures to launch online and mobile ordering. In 2008, it pioneered the Domino's Tracker, which allowed customers to view the progress of their order from receipt to preparation to baking, packaging, and delivery. When Brandon announced his departure in 2009, which didn't officially occur until 2010, Domino's had a 9 percent share of the pizza restaurant market, according to

Bloomberg Businessweek,[13] with sales of $5.6 billion, per *Pizza Today.* It was the second-largest pizza chain, with nearly 50 percent of its sales originating internationally. Just as Brandon exited, Domino's had opened its nine thousandth store worldwide.

But perhaps the biggest achievement of his time at Domino's was the complete overhaul of its namesake pizza. The recipe that had served the chain well for nearly fifty years had lost favor with customers. In fact, a consumer study from loyalty research firm Brand Keys in 2009 placed Domino's first in price and convenience against its competition, but tied for last in taste.[14] As he handed over the CEO mantle to Doyle, Brandon had just finished a complete makeover of the company's pizza, all based on input from its customers. The pizza's crust, sauce, cheese, and toppings had all been changed up in the interests of quality and flavor. And on December 27, 2009, it hit the market. Customers loved it. Brandon left Domino's for the University of Michigan on a new career high.

❝ But perhaps the biggest achievement of his time at Domino's was the complete overhaul of its namesake pizza. The recipe that had served the chain well for nearly fifty years had lost favor with customers. In fact, a consumer study from loyalty research firm Brand Keys in 2009 placed Domino's first in price and convenience against its competition, but tied for last in taste.

"Patrick Doyle is one of the most consequential restaurant executives of all time."

CHAPTER TWELVE

PATRICK DOYLE TAKES OVER AS CEO

E ven before David Brandon announced that he was leaving to head intercollegiate athletics at the University of Michigan, Patrick Doyle was stepping into the spotlight at Domino's. As early as January 2009, he was quoted in connection with the company's massive overhaul of its pizza recipe, though he didn't officially take the reins as CEO until March 8, 2009.

According to the *Wall Street Journal*, "Doyle became CEO after two of the company's worst years, and sales were still sliding."[1] Nation's Restaurant Business said that "Domino's was reeling" as Doyle took command.[2] He had been president of Domino's USA since 2007, having joined the company in 1997.[3] During his time at Domino's, he had led the company's marketing department, then international division, and then its corporate store unit, *QSR* reported.

Like his predecessor, Brandon, Doyle is an alum of the University of Michigan, where he earned an undergraduate economics degree. He then earned an MBA from the University of

Chicago. Doyle started his career at the First Chicago Bank in finance but, after five years, was encouraged by his wife to take a chance and accept an international role at InterVascular, a medical device maker, and work out of France. He came back to the US for a position at Gerber Products before joining Domino's in 1997 as the senior vice president of marketing, *Investor's Business Daily* reports.[4]

How Pizza Chains Were Faring in 2009

Nearing the end of the first decade of the 2000s, pizza had transitioned from becoming a staple in the American diet to losing ground by 2010. After gaining significant market share in the 1990s up into the 2000s, where pizza chains comprised twelve of the nation's top fast-food brands, that momentum slowed by the end of the decade, according to *QSR*.[5] The magazine reported:

> Over this century's first decade, however, pizza's momentum slowed—first to a jog, then to a crawl, and, for a time, some observers contend, even into reverse gear. In the most recent QSR 50, pizza chains held only four of the top 25 spots and seven of the top 50, with no fresh-blooded pizza chains even threatening to crack the list. More telling, the chicken category supplanted pizza as the runner-up to burgers in representation.

By 2010, *QSR* found, where pizza chains had occupied twelve of the country's top fifty quick-service spots in 2000, only seven were still listed in 2010. Some of the big names to fall off that list included Chuck E. Cheese, Round Table Pizza, Godfather's Pizza, Uno, and Pizza Inn.

It appeared that the problem wasn't so much with pizza as it was with consumer preference for food variety. Technomic reported in 2010:

A significant percentage of consumers (41 percent) are reporting that their idea of places offering "fast food" has expanded recently to include fast-casual restaurants such as Panera and full-service restaurants offering carryout and curbside service.[6]

This shift in consumer eating habits affected the fast-food industry as a whole, including Domino's. Still recovering from the video prank nightmare in 2009, Domino's hadn't yet hit on a strategy that would reverse its sales decline. According to *Nation's Restaurant News*:

Sales at the then-8,886-unit chain were weak (same-store sales at domestic locations fell a total of 10 percent between 2006 and 2008) and the brand, despite launches of new menu lines such as sandwiches and pasta, and even attempts at technological breakthroughs, such as allowing customers to order through their television sets using TiVo, failed to spur excitement among the public.[7]

But Domino's wasn't alone. Pizza Hut was also feeling the effects of declining pizza consumption and in late 2009/early 2010 was trying new tactics to jump-start sales with some success. CBS News reported that, in the first quarter of 2010, Pizza Hut had introduced a new flat price of $10—"Any pizza, any size, any toppings, $10."[8] That offer, backed with a sizable advertising campaign and a foray into baked pasta dishes and eight flavors of chicken wings, was reversing the course. In the first quarter of 2010, Pizza Hut achieved 5 percent sales growth, versus a decline of 12 percent in 2009. *Nation's Restaurant News* also reported that, in 2009, Pizza Hut launched an app for ordering pizza that had boosted sales for the chain by more than $1 million in its first three months.[9]

Domino's was still working through what its turnaround strategy might consist of. To help, it was conducting market research to better understand its customers. What it heard likely wasn't what it was hoping for, however: "Focus groups were taking Domino's to task, criticizing the pizza for lacking flavor and arriving on crusts that tasted like cardboard."[10]

The good news is that feedback sparked a big idea the company could use to effectively relaunch its whole brand. To pull away from its delivery focus of the past, Domino's would reformulate its whole pizza recipe, developing a pizza with an entirely new taste, texture, and appearance. This overhaul began under Brandon, though Doyle had certainly been heavily involved, and it was completed under his watch.

> Domino's had just survived six straight quarters of declining revenue when Doyle took to the airwaves to announce the new recipe on December 16, 2009. The company was going all in on remaking its core product and, as *Smart Business* reported, it had no backup plan if the new pizza recipe failed.

This new launch also involved Domino's taking responsibility for its past pizza problems. Doyle, as CEO, filmed a four-minute documentary of the process (watch at http://pizzaturnaround.com/) and several thirty-second commercials in which he spoke personally to Domino's customers, apologizing. Domino's had just survived six straight quarters of declining revenue[11] when Doyle took to the airwaves to announce the new recipe on December 16, 2009. The company was going all in on remaking its core product and, as *Smart Business* reported, it had no backup plan if the new pizza recipe failed.[12]

Doyle's Early Priorities

When Doyle took charge at Domino's, he laid out three main goals for the company, according to *QSR*:

1. Become the #1 pizza company in the world
2. Provide its franchisees with the best possible return on their investment by creating a "dramatically better" experience for its customers
3. Put a leadership team in place that could help the company achieve even better results going forward[13]

To do that, he promised customers transparency, to rebuild the trust he believed they may have lost through the years as its recipe became less and less like the original. His appearances in TV ads were an effort to do just that—communicate openly and honestly with Domino's customers, old and new.

Introducing an entirely new recipe was a linchpin of its climb to number one in the industry. That step was bold and unexpected, and certainly shook things up for quite some time. It also increased sales.

Investing more heavily in technology was another tactic Doyle used to support Domino's efforts to improve operations and generate more revenue. Doyle told *Forbes*:

> "We decided to bring all of our technology development in house, not just individual aspects of it," Doyle said. "We made the decision between us that there would be a real competitive advantage in technology, but we needed to start bringing it inside. And we had to figure out how you recruit great technology talent into a pizza company. Would we be able to do it?"[14]

Brandon had already started driving Domino's down that road during his tenure, making Domino's "the first in the pizza business to lead with technology for simplifying, streamlining, and democratizing its crucial ordering and delivery operations—even though they weren't sure back in 2009 exactly what that would mean."[15] Per *DBusiness*, together, Brandon and Doyle had "decided that Domino's would somehow have to leverage technology to spark growth."[16]

> "We didn't know what it would look like yet, but we had to be in the center of [technology], understanding what was going on and creating a competitive advantage by being ahead of the curve," Doyle recalls.

Another wise move was deciding to bring technology and innovation in-house:

> "We decided to bring all of our technology development in-house, not just individual aspects of it," Doyle explains. "We made the decision between us that there would be a real competitive advantage in technology, but we needed to start bringing it inside."[17]

Innovation and reliance on technology would become the cornerstone of Doyle's time at Domino's, which ended in June 2018, when he retired. After taking over during a tumultuous time for Domino's, Doyle successfully righted the ship. In his eight years as CEO, Doyle helped Domino's double its market share and increase the company's share price more than 1,900 percent, as the stock price rose from $13.74 on March 8, 2010, to $282.17 on June 30, 2018.

"We said our old pizza wasn't very good. . . .
This was back in 2009, 2010 when banks
were going under. Consumers were just
feeling like they were being lied to. It was
a breath of fresh air that someone was
willing to tell them the truth."

—**RUSSELL WEINER,**
Domino's Chief Operating Officer

CHAPTER THIRTEEN

CHANGING THE PIZZA RECIPE

To understand how Domino's managed to climb out of the hole it was in back in 2007 and 2008, it's important to study the decision to create an entirely new pizza recipe from scratch. It was a risky move, to be sure, but Brandon and Doyle were confident that they needed to focus there to regenerate sales. After all, the company's operating processes were well honed, they had skilled talent on board, so reworking the core product was really the last piece of the puzzle to be addressed.

As Domino's exited the Great Recession of the 2000s, its position as pizza delivery leader was holding strong. But it was losing ground on other fronts to category leaders Pizza Hut and Papa John's, *QSR* reported.[1] The problem, Brand Keys research firm uncovered, was that the taste of its pizza wasn't winning any awards. Actually, as you've already heard, it tied (with Chuck E. Cheese) for last place for taste among major pizza chains in 2009. In fact, if subjects knew the pizza was from Domino's, they actually reported liking it less than if they didn't know who made it.[2] Clearly, Domino's brand image had taken a big hit. It needed a makeover. Sure, it was the leader in price and convenience, but losing the taste war put Domino's in a precarious position long term.

Sales in 2008 were $3.037 billion and fell by the smallest margin, to $3.03 in 2009. Of greater concern was that the chain had posted seven negative quarters in a row, per researcher Technomic in *Adweek*.[3] Domino's stock price hit a record low of $2.83 in November 2008.[4]

Trying a New Ad Campaign

Before Domino's even considered jumping into a massive recipe renovation, it first tried to solve the problem of the evaporating sales with marketing. Trying to leverage its heritage as a delivery pioneer, Domino's wanted to remind its customers why they'd always bought from Domino's —reliable, fast delivery. So, in early 2008, it launched a new promotional campaign.

Doyle told *Smart Business* what the new ad campaign was all about:

> "We had launched a new ad campaign called 'You Got 30,' which kind of took us back to our roots," says Doyle, the president and CEO of Domino's Pizza Inc. "While we weren't guaranteeing anyone a 30-minute delivery, we were reminding them that most of the time, they'll get their pizza in 30 minutes. The campaign emphasized how Domino's saves you time and what you could do with that 30 minutes."

The campaign fell on deaf ears. Consumers had heard it all before.

"They simply did not care," Doyle says. "The consumers who already used us because they appreciated the convenience already knew what we were telling them. Those that didn't, who said the convenience factor was great but we needed better food, it didn't change their minds about anything. So it was right then, in March 2008, about two months after we launched that ad campaign, that we decided we needed to go back to the drawing board with our pizza."[5]

Unable to move the needle by pushing its delivery capabilities, Domino's had little choice but to look inward at its product as the source of a potential solution to its declining revenue. Its pizza was really the only aspect of its operation that it hadn't improved or changed much.

> Unable to move the needle by pushing its delivery capabilities, Domino's had little choice but to look inward at its product as the source of a potential solution to its declining revenue. Its pizza was really the only aspect of its operation that it hadn't improved or changed much.

Cost-Cutting Gone Awry

It turns out, Domino's pizza recipe in 2008 looked and tasted nothing like the original.

Sparked by the economic recession in the 2000s, a lot of attention was paid in 2005 and 2006 to how to improve profits at a time when fewer customers were buying pizzas, McIntyre explains. In trying to come up with new ways to modify the pizza to reduce costs, different stores had tried various tactics. One group tweaked the dough recipe to get costs down. Another tweaked the sauce recipe, while others tried different cheeses and pepperonis. While each individual tweak may not have had much of an impact on the overall pizza taste, together, those small changes resulted in a pizza "no one liked anymore," McIntyre reported. Sales dropped.

In looking at social media and reading customer care messages, it became clear that the problem was with the product. "Domino's isn't like it used to be," many customers were reporting. Management couldn't disagree. The Domino's pizza recipe, through several iterations, had gone too far afield. It was time to get back on track with a pizza that would once again win national taste tests. "No one would believe it was 'new and improved,' unless it was truly better tasting," Russell Weiner, chief operating officer and president of the Americas at Domino's, explained.[6]

To generate new revenue while the company worked on getting the new pizza recipe right, Domino's launched other new products, Weiner said, including sandwiches, lava cake, and some new specialty pizzas. "They brought in new customers and bought us time to launch our new pizza," he said.

Change Gets Underway

It was in 2008 that Domino's secretly began researching, testing, and tweaking a potential new pizza recipe. The *Ann Arbor News* reported:

Domino's spent 2 years testing "dozens of cheeses, 15 sauces, and nearly 50 crust seasoning blends and researched every possible combination with customers who order from us all the time and customers who haven't tried us in years," chief marketing officer Russell Weiner said in a statement.[7]

The company turned to its regular customers and those who had all but given up on Domino's to taste test its newest recipe. Domino's "researched every possible combination," it said. Weiner laid out the entire process[8] in a presentation (see Figure 1), starting with reformulating the dough for its crust, followed by reinventing its sauce, then cheese, then crust style, then creating myriad combinations, followed by user testing.

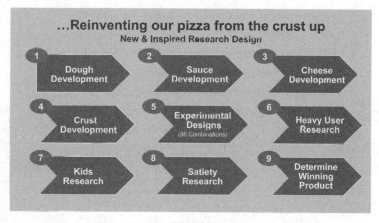

FIGURE 1

Doyle described the process similarly in a *Smart Business* interview:

"We did every possible kind of research," Doyle says. "We were doing qualitative research like focus groups, where you're getting people into a room and having them help you get a sense for where the opportunities were. Those were the comments you ended up seeing in the commercials themselves. But then, we also went out and tested every possible ingredient change, every combination of new sauces, crusts and cheeses, until we thought we had it optimized. Then, we took the new pizza ideas to our most loyal customers to see if they'd appreciate the change. We took it to people who weren't doing business with us. We went to kids, we went to every possible demographic group and kept testing it."[9]

Ultimately, the key changes Domino's made to its pizza included:

- A "garlic-seasoned crust with parsley baked to a golden brown."
- A "sweeter, bolder tomato sauce with a medley of herbs and a red pepper kick." Doyle said the new sauce has 40 percent more herbs.
- Mozzarella cheese "flavored with just a hint of provolone," which is shredded instead of diced.[10]

"We did taste tests against the competition and won," Weiner said. In a nationwide road show consisting of blind taste tests, Domino's won hands down. The results were 994 to 6. It was clear they had a winner. Once Domino's had reinvented its product, the next task was retraining everyone—including all of its franchisees—in how to make a pizza properly using its new ingredients.

Franchisee Training Begins

The new pizza was ready for rollout by the end of 2009, but first employees had to be educated. According to the *Ann Arbor News*, during the first two weeks of December 2009 Domino's spent two hundred thousand hours retraining workers at its nearly five thousand stores.[11] *Smart Business* detailed that process as well:

> In December 2009, Domino's had to retrain 4,900 franchises on how to make a pizza. Corporate leadership had to ensure that the old ingredients ran out and new ingredients were stocked as close as possible to the changeover period, which was the week between Christmas and New Year's Day, when Domino's rolled out their first ad campaign touting the new pizza.

It was a massive logistical balancing act, and it had to be carried out in the span of several weeks.

> "We trained a hundred trainers, they each had 50 stores to cover, and there are typically two to three people in each store who are making the pizzas," Doyle says. "We'd have the trainers organize the pizza makers into groups of 10 to 15 people per day. Over the span of a couple of weeks, each trainer probably trained about 150 people. You just get the people into a store and go to work. You show them how to do it, and you don't let them leave until you're confident they can do it right."

The scope of the transition didn't allow for a completely clean break between old and new. There was a period of about a week just before Christmas when a given store could have been selling the old pizza or the new.[12]

Once ready to debut its new creation, Domino's led with a self-deprecating advertising campaign that laid bare all of the harsh comments it had received about its pizza. Investing $75 million in a six-week campaign consisting of fifteen- and thirty-second TV ads and sixty-second radio and web spots, Domino's timed the ads with its new pizza's debut.[13] It also offered a money-back guarantee to reduce any perceived risk of giving the company another chance. The *Washington Post* called it the mea culpa campaign.[14]

It started with the "Show Us Your Pizza" campaign, says Weiner. Domino's asked customers to send in photos of the pizzas they received. They got thirty thousand. "Most companies would show only the great-looking pizzas," said Weiner,[15] "but we took the opposite approach. We showed a bad pizza and promised it wouldn't happen again." That move earned the company respect and trust, he said.

That honesty and transparency about its failing was phase 2 of Domino's new campaign.

In the final phase of the new pizza rollout, Domino's wanted to show how all aspects of the pizza ordering and eating experience had been improved, Weiner said. So the company showed how to more easily order a pizza, how it would be delivered, how the pizza tracker worked, and its new loyalty program. "We were thinking of ourselves as a pizza company that overdelivers on pizza," said Weiner.

Back on Top

The good news is that Domino's risk-taking paid off. "The product cost more money, but the system was all in," said Weiner. Even before sales numbers began reporting, customer satisfaction results were way up. Domino's "carried out blind taste tests with 1,800 random pizza consumers, coming out on top and beating both Pizza Hut and Papa John's by a wide margin," the Motley Fool reported.[16]

> " The product cost more money, but the system was all in," said Weiner. Even before sales numbers began reporting, customer satisfaction results were way up. Domino's "carried out blind taste tests with 1,800 random pizza consumers, coming out on top and beating both Pizza Hut and Papa John's by a wide margin."

Bloomberg reported that, by February 2010, little more than two months after the introduction, Domino's was selling so much pizza that it was three days away from running out of pepperoni.[17] In addition to seeing a huge surge in demand, Domino's was getting two thumbs up from its customers. The *Ann Arbor News* reported that Domino's own research found that the percentage of consumers who said they would "definitely purchase this pizza in the future" went up 25 percent thanks to the new recipe. And sales were also up. At stores open at least a year, sales improved 14.3 percent in the first quarter, 8.8 percent in the second quarter, and 11.7 percent in the third quarter, which was a monumental win.[18]

Weiner reported in his presentation that, by 2012, Domino's had hit #1 in pizza taste and was the fastest-growing quick-serve restaurant concept, with US same-store sales growth of 17 percent between 2009–2012.[19]

The pizza industry immediately took note. In a *Time* magazine article,[20] Barclays Capital analyst Jeffrey Bernstein credited Domino's for turning in a "banner year" in pizza delivery, a "mature concept" in a "mature U.S. market" in which 1 percent to 3 percent growth is the norm. The industry's leading trade publication, *Pizza Today*, named Domino's the pizza chain of the year for the second time. Domino's was back.

Not only that, its apology had earned respect from the market. "'Doing a Domino's' became code for looking at ourselves critically and finding improvement opportunities," McIntyre says. Once again, Domino's was in growth mode.

"They offer an everyday value and a good quality product and a good experience in ordering and reordering. The convenience of having it ordered with just a push of a button or two and having it delivered to you is really compelling."

—ALEXANDER SLAGLE,

analyst with the Jefferies investment firm to the *Los Angeles Times*

CHAPTER FOURTEEN

BECOMING THE "TECH COMPANY THAT SELLS PIZZA"

Having survived the pizza industry's lean times in the early 2000s, Domino's new pizza product fueled significant growth for the company for several years, supported by a sizable investment in behind-the-scenes technology. In fact, US digital sales—meaning originating online or through its mobile app—at Domino's went from 0 percent to more than 65 percent in about a decade, Domino's reported to investors in August 2019.[1] Its emphasis on digital growth was also paying off beyond the US borders. More than 75 percent of Domino's international markets featured online ordering. The company's emphasis on technology innovation helped Domino's achieve more than half of all global retail sales in 2018 from digital channels, it reported.[2]

But Domino's had really started to look at building a robust technology foundation as far back as 2001.

Keeping Tech Development In-House

It was between 2001 and 2003 that Domino's rolled out a proprietary single point-of-sale system, called Pulse, which franchisees were required to adopt. That decision was noteworthy because of the trickle-down impact it had on all of its franchisees, *Restaurant Business* explained.

> Franchises have long preferred single systems, but have given franchisees the ability to shop for their own systems in the name of cost cutting. Domino's took the controversial step of forcing a single system on its operators, one it developed in-house. Franchisees sued. Domino's won.
>
> Today, it's hard to find anybody who disagrees with the system. The single POS system has made it much easier for Domino's to add technology and gives the company more information on its operators' performance.[3]

There had been five or six different systems in use at difference franchisees, says Tim McIntyre, but no one overarching platform. The problem was, CEO Ritch Allison explained, that "off-the-shelf systems didn't work" for Domino's. It wasn't that the company was choosing between an existing system and developing one on its own; there simply wasn't anything that could do what Domino's wanted to do. So they built it themselves.

Bringing the POS development in-house gave Domino's control over its performance, as well as control over the time required to add functionality or fix bugs—the company known for speedy deliveries works as hard to be efficient and fast throughout its entire operation. "Working in-house speeds the process," *Nation's Restaurant News* confirmed.[4]

Its POS system allowed the company to amass detailed information about its customers, to help its franchisees better serve them. To that end, Domino's "invested in data-driven personalization, a move that began with bringing point-of-sales systems in-house and developing customers' 'Pizza Profiles,' which put customer preferences and payment information behind the mobile app."[5] But personalization capabilities came after Domino's realized that it previously took twenty-five steps to place an order online, resulting in many abandoned shopping carts. It went to work streamlining and simplifying its whole order process. Perhaps more importantly, Domino's could control who had access to that detailed customer data, which provided a significant competitive advantage.

The company's success with developing and managing its POS using internal resources likely perpetuated the belief that keeping technology projects in-house was a smart choice. So, when the decision was made in 2009 to rebuild the company's website and data centers, Domino's again decided to trust its skilled in-house staffers with the work to be done.[6]

The Focus on Digital

Domino's had long made a concerted effort to drive digital innovation at the company, actually launching online and mobile ordering back in 2007 and being one of the first food companies to debut online ordering capability.[7] It was a pioneer in online ordering and wanted to stay in the lead.

At the same time as Domino's was introducing digital ordering, it was hard at work developing a food delivery industry first—a pizza order tracker. This innovation was in response to Domino's discovery of the "emotional roller coaster of delivery,"

McIntyre explains. There is the emotional high when someone suggests, "Let's get a pizza!" Followed by the low of waiting for it, worrying about when it will arrive and if the delivery will be correct, he says, and then the high of hearing the doorbell ring. That emotional low point, when there is "a void in information"—when the customer is left not knowing when their order will get there—can lead to feelings of negativity, McIntyre reports. So Domino's decided to build something to fill in that void and ensure that customers were constantly updated with information—"to smooth out that rollercoaster."

> **Domino's had long made a concerted effort to drive digital innovation at the company, actually launching online and mobile ordering back in 2007 and being one of the first food companies to debut online ordering capability.**

A year later, in 2008, Domino's rolled it out. According to Domino's, the Domino's Tracker™ "allows Domino's Pizza customers to follow the progress of their order online, from the time they click the 'Place Order' button (or hang up the phone), until the order is delivered." By mid-March 2008, one million customers had used the Domino's Tracker, *QSR* reported.[8]

That same year, 2008, Domino's also launched its Pizza Builder online tool. According to *Adweek*, the online app, built by Crispin Porter + Bogusky, lets users put together their own pizza digitally, name it, and then have it made and delivered to their door.[9] The creative pros at Crispin recognized the power of such a tool and applauded Domino's for paving the way. *Adweek* reported, "For Jeff Benjamin, the interactive creative director at Crispin, the web application that debuted early this year is a sign of where digital design is headed. Rather than craft a one-off website, he said, advertisers want to build brand loyalty by providing utilities that both improve people's lives in some small way—even if it's simply a tool for customizing pizza—and directly pad corporate bottom lines."[10]

The pizza builder led the way for several years, until 2014, when Domino's released an iPad app with a new, more realistic custom version. Domino's heralded it as "the coolest technology we have launched since Domino's Tracker."

With all the resources focused on building new digital apps and customer-facing technologies, it was clear Domino's was all in on digital. In 2011, they said as much, setting a goal to move the business from just over 20 percent in digital sales to more than 50 percent by 2015, it reported in a Shorty Awards entry.[11] That shift was important because Domino's had learned that the average online buyer was spending $2 more than buyers who ordered by phone or in person.[12] There was money online, and Domino's went after it with a vengeance, ultimately aiming for 100 percent digital orders.

In a *Forbes* article, then-CEO Doyle said, "Fundamentally, we are on a path to take all orders digitally." This means:

> The company's implementation of automated phone orders via artificial intelligence assistant DOM should further grow its digital ordering business beyond the current 65 percent. More

digital sales typically mean higher checks and better operational efficiency. According to research from analysts at BTIG, traditional phone/counter orders cost at least a dollar's worth of an employee's time, while each digital order costs about 25 cents.[13]

By 2012, driving customers online wasn't just a way to drive down costs, it was a necessity to capture more business. Promoting online ordering, advertising online and via cell phones was all resulting in higher sales. NPD research[14] reported that online marketing influenced a restaurant visit for 38 percent of smartphone users. That push to digital ordering continues. "Today, customers can order through Apple TV, Google Home, Amazon Echo, Ford Sync, SMS, Samsung Smart TVs, smartwatches, an in-app voice assistant, and other emerging platforms, as well as via Tweets, Slack, and Facebook messenger."[15]

A New Mindset

It was around 2012 that Domino's began thinking of itself more as an e-commerce company than a quick-serve restaurant, according to a *Forbes* interview with Kelly Garcia, Domino's senior vice president of e-commerce development and emerging technologies. Garcia reported that delivering a world-class e-commerce experience to Domino's customers would require buy-in at all levels of the company, from the board to the CEO to senior leaders, on down to franchisees. So, in 2012, Garcia and Dennis Maloney, Domino's chief digital officer, presented to the board of directors the threats Domino's was currently facing. Additionally, the duo "introduced the idea that to survive, they had to start thinking of themselves as an 'e-commerce company that happens to sell pizza.'"[16]

The CEO was already on board, so with the board's blessing, "the technology plan was funded." On top of the major investment in technology, however, the impact was also being felt internally, Ritch Allison says.[17] "Where decision-making used to be based more on gut feel or on the loudest voice, Domino's could now use data-driven decision-making" across nearly all facets of the company's operations. From pricing to ad messaging to where to locate new stores or when to open them, Domino's could mine the data it had gathered to make better-informed decisions.

It also fueled a "fail fast mentality," says McIntyre. When someone comes up with an idea, it is discussed, a small test is run, and if results suggest it has potential, the company does a market test. "We do a lot of A/B testing," McIntyre says. "We're not afraid to fail, so we test a lot. If you don't test, you don't innovate."

Domino's Major Technology Advances

Beginning in 2012, the work to become an e-commerce powerhouse began, and it was immediately apparent how serious Domino's was about it. In 2013, Domino's made good on its plan to make pizza ordering much simpler for its customers. Its Pizza Profiles capability was an enhanced online ordering feature that gave customers the ability to save information from orders or retrieve past records, rather than having to reenter everything. Pizza Profiles made it possible to reduce the number of clicks from twenty-five to five, and complete their order in a matter of seconds.

The following year, they kicked the ease of ordering up a notch with Dom, "a Siri-like voice-activated personal assistant that lets users order pizza with just a few words," according to DigiDay.[18] By April 2015, Domino's reported that more than five hundred thousand orders had been placed through Dom.

Between 2014 and 2015, Domino's launched AnyWare, which is a suite of ordering technology that provides customers with fifteen different ways to order a pizza digitally. Essentially, the ability to order from anywhere, anytime, using any device, Domino's promised. The company explained it this way in an awards entry:

> To get more people ordering Domino's online we brought ordering to the devices and platforms people already use every day rather than making them come to us. This new suite of ordering technology was named Domino's AnyWare and includes ordering with a tweet, a text, Ford Sync, Smart TV's, and smart watches. Each new way to order was introduced with its own press release, which drove to DominosAnyWare.com where people could learn about these new ways to order. Then in Q3 of 2015, a national TV campaign featured celebrities, with expertise in each platform, arguing that their way to order was indeed best.

Further refining its personalization efforts, Domino's introduced the Easy Order button in 2015. "An Easy Order is your favorite food order bundled with your preferred payment method, order type (delivery or carryout), and address or favorite store," said Domino's.

That year, it also unveiled "the ultimate pizza delivery vehicle"—the DXP, the "cheese-lover's Batmobile."[19] "We built a car to deliver pizzas because that's how obsessed we are," says McIntyre. The DXP is a custom-designed one-person car with space behind the driver's seat for a four-hundred-degree warming oven and a rack next to it for food and drink delivery. With a Chevy Spark as its base, the DXP can hold up to eighty pizzas. As of 2019, 150 cars had been sold and built.

> " We built a car to deliver pizzas because that's how obsessed we are," says McIntyre. The DXP is a custom-designed one-person car with space behind the driver's seat for a four-hundred-degree warming oven and a rack next to it for food and drink delivery. With a Chevy Spark as its base, the DXP can hold up to eighty pizzas.

Domino's new rewards program, called Piece of the Pie, was also introduced in 2015. The digital loyalty program rewards customers who order online, crediting them with ten points for every order valued at over $10. After six orders, the customer earns a free medium, two-topping pizza. What better way to encourage customers to head online to place an order, rather than call or walk in, than to reward them for their behavior.

Next, Domino's unveiled Zero Click Ordering, which was an effort to make getting a pizza delivered as easy as humanly possible. With Zero Click Ordering, Domino's customers set up an account and specify their Easy Order—their go-to pizza. Then, when they launch the Easy Order app, in ten seconds their order is placed and is on its way to arriving at their doorstep.

With technology woven throughout nearly every aspect of its business, Domino's appeared to turn its attention to expanding its footprint in nontraditional ways. In 2018, the company launched Domino's Hotspots, allowing customers to order deliveries to these meet-up spots, like parks or youth sports fields, that do not have traditional delivery addresses. When a customer orders online, they can choose a Hotspot location for the delivery, just as they can choose their home or work address.

Domino's continues to test new technology and potential services. In 2017, it announced it was working on driverless delivery, ordering through connected-car touchscreens, and automated decision-making through command-based apps, *Crain's Detroit Business*[20] reported. By talking to store managers, to learn their pain points, Allison said, Domino's uncovered other opportunities to automate other aspects of the business. For example, store managers who have to do inventory at the end of the day, at 2 a.m., but really want to go home to bed, can now use a voice-activated inventory app that helps them get the task done in twenty minutes instead of two hours, he says.

Automated kiosks are now in four hundred US stores, where customers can check in and pay there, saving them wait time and reducing reliance on counter labor.[21] And, in 2019, Domino's opened its Innovation Garage, consisting of a life-size store built inside its headquarters. The goal in setting it up was to allow elements of the store to be torn apart to find efficiencies within, explained McIntyre.

Tech Investment Pays Off

Despite some of the market skepticism heard in the early 2000s regarding Domino's foray into technology, with 20/20 hindsight, most analysts agree that the bet paid off. It was a smart strategy at a time when its competition was more focused on other areas of the business, from delivery to store expansion to marketing cleverness and menu additions. Domino's focused on innovation and improvement with a single-minded determination.

By 2012, only a few years after its new pizza made headlines, Domino's surpassed $1 billion in digital sales in one year, according to an investor presentation. Thirty-five percent of its US orders were placed online. By 2013, at its Ann Arbor headquarters, the largest department in the company was technology, accounting for about 170 jobs out of 550, or 31 percent.[22] By 2018, the department made up 50 percent of the whole headquarters crew, reported DigiDay. Two years later, more than 50 percent of its sales came via digital platforms.[23] And according to CNBC, of all pizzas ordered online, 31 percent were from Domino's.[24] As Jonathan Maze at *Nation's Restaurant News* summarizes,[25] investing in technology is how "Domino's became the most technologically adept chain in the restaurant business—one that has revolutionized the way concepts think of technology and its potential to bring in business."

"The Grubhubs and Uber
Eats of the world will
[challenge] us. . . . We
need to keep pushing
ourselves to maintain our
advantage."

—ART D'ELIA,
Domino's Chief Brand and Innovation Officer

CHAPTER FIFTEEN

CREATIVE ADVERTISING

Domino's success in 2010 and 2011 was based on developing and introducing entirely new brand positioning, which was built on an entirely new pizza. This was an extremely risky move for an established pizza empire. Imagine consumer reaction if Starbuck's suddenly told everyone that it was embarrassed by how bad its coffee was (which isn't true), or if Ben & Jerry's came out and said its ice cream didn't taste as good as it possibly could (hard to imagine)?! For a company to malign its own creation was certainly a new marketing approach.

Chief Marketing Officer Russell Weiner wasn't worried though, because he knew it was what needed to be done to reverse three years of same-store sales decline. The company had done its research—and lots of it—and knew exactly how to proceed.

At a time when consumers were skeptical and wary, Domino's had an opportunity to step up and be transparent and vulnerable. Weiner told *Forbes* magazine:

Our strategy tapped into a consumer insight that had nothing to do with pizza. At the time we were doing the brand positioning, all these banks were going under and folks were asking for bailouts and the bailouts were created by the politicians and funded by the middle class. Consumers were just looking for people to stop lying to them, stop ripping them off and just be truthful and transparent. That was a societal finding, not specifically related to pizza, obviously. But we felt that if we could make it part of our brand strategy, our communication would help us take off because it was something that wasn't just applicable to pizza consumers, it was applicable to everybody.[1]

Although at the core was a pizza transformation, the process began with Domino's examining its own messaging.

Transparency as a Brand Strategy

In 2009, Americans were experiencing an era of rapid social media adoption, according to Pew research, which had begun around 2005. From 2005 to 2010, the percentage of American adults who used social media rose from 7 percent to 46 percent; by 2015, that number was 65 percent.[2] That shift in news and information sources called into question the accuracy and reliability of what was being shared online. What was true? Who could be trusted? How could you tell? No one seemed sure. It was hard to know, which fueled greater skepticism and mistrust, not just of the media but of everyone.

As the new pizza was being launched, Weiner explained in an Entrepreneurship Hour presentation at the University of Michigan[3] that people believed that "no one would tell you the truth," citing Michigan auto execs flying into Washington, DC, in private jets to ask for bailouts, banks going under, and families losing their homes. According to the 2010 Edelman Trust Barometer of college-educated adults age twenty-five and up, who earned in the top quartile for their age and country, the credibility of corporate or product advertising was low, at 17 percent.[4] Perhaps of greater significance for Domino's, however, was that the Trust Barometer showed that trust and transparency were as important to corporate reputation as the quality of products and services. This insight reinforces the sense that Domino's was on the right track by shifting its communication message to one of transparency and by investing heavily in redesigning its core product to ensure it was of superior quality.

Americans "wanted people to tell them the truth," Weiner explains, and Domino's had a hard truth to admit about itself—the company's pizza "wasn't very good." The collision of those two tensions could relieve the pent-up brand, customer, and cultural tension that existed and help to "amplify Domino's message" if the company got it right, Weiner says.

<blockquote>
Americans "wanted people to tell them the truth," Weiner explains, and Domino's had a hard truth to admit about itself—the company's pizza "wasn't very good." The collision of those two tensions could relieve the pent-up brand, customer, and cultural tension that existed and help to "amplify Domino's message" if the company got it right.
</blockquote>

Producing an Epic Turnaround

Domino's $75 million ad campaign announcing its new pizza was actually less than the previous year's budget, less than Pizza Hut's, and less than Papa John's,[5] Weiner stated. "We didn't do it with more money, and I think that just shows the power of the message."

Domino's new tagline, rolled out in conjunction with its new recipe, was, "Oh Yes We Did," which became the company's rally cry in response to surprised reactions from the market.

Weiner suggested thinking about the company's advertising campaign as a play in four acts.

Act I: January 2010

Domino's explains in its first round of advertising, "We listened to our toughest critics and they inspired us to reinvent our pizza from the crust up!" Admitting its pizza had been bad was difficult but necessary, according to Weiner. But that was just the first six weeks of its rollout activities.

Not all ad gurus were in favor of Domino's approach. *Ad Age* gave it a 1.5-star review and commented, "It is one thing to eat a little crow and another to overdose on sodium pentothal."[6] However, it did give credit for putting it all on the line, calling the turnaround campaign "arguably one of the riskiest marketing campaigns of all time." It is risky because consumers may not hear the whole message, as a *Washington Post* article explains:

"Some people are going to hear only part of the message"—Domino's stinks—"and not hear the part about how they're going to get better," says Bill Benoit, a communications professor at Ohio University. Thus, apology ads can reinforce negative perceptions and raise awareness of them among people who've never tried, or even heard of, the product.[7]

The *New Republic*, another skeptic, gave the ads an A in theory and an F in practice, saying, "You come away thinking, 'Wow, even the people at Domino's think Domino's is bad.'"[8]

But some ad industry observers gave kudos to Domino's for demonstrating how far it was willing to go to show its customers that it heard them, and that it was taking action.

The advertising drives you to the "Pizza Turnaround" landing page where you can view a four-and-a-half minute behind-the-scenes documentary. It already has more than a half million hits and has been spoofed multiple times. Hey, if they're talking about you, they're thinking about you. The campaign has also gained press attention, with mentions on broadcasts including *Mad Money*, *The Colbert Report*, Oprah Radio and *The Early Show*.[9]

The next phase was demonstrating that the pizza was actually delicious.

Act II: February–March 2010

It has long been known that testimonials are powerful marketing tools, when you can get them. So Domino's took another chance, returning to previous focus group participants who had expressed how much they disliked the company's pizza. With camera rolling, store managers went door-to-door to the focus group critics and asked them to taste the new-and-improved Domino's. The reactions were marketing gold. Says Weiner of the videos, "We faced our toughest critics and they loved our inspired new pizza!"

To support this next phase with double-click marketing, Domino's put a live Twitter feed on the company's website homepage to show what people were saying about the pizza in real time. That effort generated several million hits on its own.

Act III: July–August 2010

A few months later, Domino's followed up with ads that proclaimed, in essence, "Our pizza is so good, we don't need fancy photography or food stylists to make it more tempting." Then it asked customers to shoot photos of their pizzas and send them in. As of 2015, Domino's was using only customer photography in its marketing. The company had received more than thirty thousand photos for its website, reported the *Ann Arbor News*.[10]

> It asked customers to shoot photos of their pizzas and send them in. As of 2015, Domino's was using only customer photography in its marketing. The company had received more than thirty thousand photos.

Act IV: September 2010–

Instead of claiming a win at that point, Domino's stayed humble and expressed its commitment to continuing to listen and improve. By late 2010, Domino's was delivering one million pizzas a day. But it knew that continuing to grow would require identifying its weak spots and addressing them.

The New Domino's

Having regained the footing lost in the early years of the 2000s, Domino's continued to keep customers on their toes. The company dropped "Pizza" from its name and refreshed its logo—the first time in about fifteen years. The innovation continued, with Domino's celebrating it at each step.

In 2012, Domino's launched Think Oven, a Facebook platform where customers and fans could submit their suggestions for improving the business. Building on its message that Domino's is always listening to its customers, Think Oven was a way to tap into the creativity of people who knew the company and its products well. A *Fast Company* article explained the Think Oven concept:

> [Individuals] can submit their suggestions in two categories: the Idea Box (for general ideas, e.g. new menu items, tips for going green, etc.) and Current Project (for specific things Domino's needs help with, e.g. this month's topic of "New Domino's Uniforms"). The best idea under Current Project is handpicked after the deadline for submissions and will be rewarded with $500.[11]

Domino's has also worked hard to stay abreast of the latest thinking and technology, as well as monitoring trending ideas and news. So, when emojis were becoming popular with the rising use of text messaging, it introduced pizza order by emoji. After Domino's developed an app that connects a customer "easy order" to the app, customers could suddenly have a pizza delivered to their door simply by texting a pepperoni pizza slice emoji.

The list of Domino's innovations over the next few years included:

- a self-driving delivery robot
- a wedding registry
- a Paving for Pizza initiative to pay for local potholes
- offering rewards points on rival pizzeria pizzas
- Domino's Tinder ads, which showed "hot slices" as potential love matches
- delivering the first-ever pizza by drone in New Zealand

Although Domino's may have spent less than the competition at the start of its turnaround, by 2017, Domino's had the third-highest advertising spend in the US, reports Statista.[12] Its creative advertising approach certainly earned the company attention, initially, then respect, and then sales. Lots of sales.

> " The list of Domino's innovations over the next few years included a self-driving delivery robot, a wedding registry, creating a Paving for Pizza initiative to pay for local potholes, and offering rewards points on rival pizzeria pizzas that also included the first Domino's Tinder ads.

"Domino's Pizza claims it has surpassed Pizza Hut to become the largest pizza chain in the world."

CHAPTER SIXTEEN

DOMINO'S CLAIMS THE #1 SPOT

Having recovered from the pizza drought caused by the Great Recession, and then effectively helping to rejuvenate the entire pizza industry, Domino's set its sights on becoming an industry leader. It had come close before, and, as of 2016, Domino's was ranked second behind Pizza Hut, with a nearly $4 billion sales gap between them, according to *Pizza Today*'s Top Pizza Companies list for 2017,[1]

Although $4 billion is a large gap to close, Domino's had considerable momentum behind them. And, in just a year, Domino's reduced that deficit, in part because Pizza Hut's sales also fell. By 2017, Domino's had reported global sales of $12,252,100,000 and Pizza Hut had $12,034,000,000, landing Domino's for the first time ahead in the rankings.[2]

• • •

> " Although $4 billion is a large gap to close, Domino's had considerable momentum behind them. And, in just a year, Domino's reduced that deficit, in part because Pizza Hut's sales also fell. By 2017, Domino's had reported global sales of $12,252,100,000 and Pizza Hut had $12,034,000,000, landing Domino's for the first time ahead in the rankings.

2018 Top 100 Pizza Companies

When Domino's announced its fourth quarter earnings for fiscal year 2017, on February 20, 2018, it called itself "the largest pizza company in the world based on global retail sales." So, how had Domino's made such a big leap in such a short amount of time? The traction had been building gradually for many quarters, but it was the last few weeks in 2017 that propelled the company atop the pizza chain leaderboard.

A Quarter-by-Quarter Analysis

In the first quarter of 2017, Domino's had strong same-store sales growth globally. Domestically, growth hit 10.2 percent.[3] Meanwhile, at Pizza Hut, a division of Yum Brands, system sales were down 7 percent.[4]

Things went downhill from there during the second quarter for Pizza Hut. *QSR* magazine reported that, in May 2017, as Pizza Hut's US sales "plummeted 7 percent, Yum! revealed a $130 million plan to transform the brand."[5] This plan involved allocating funds to high priority weaknesses within its operations:

> The investment will go toward upgrading restaurant equipment to improve operations, accelerate improvements in restaurant technology, enhance digital and ecommerce capabilities, and boost advertising dollars, Yum! executives said in a conference call Wednesday.[6]

In return for the $130 million investment, Pizza Hut franchisees agreed to "follow all national price points through 2019 and to increase their contribution to the ad fund," *Nation's Restaurant News* reported.[7]

CNBC reported, also in May, that the gap between Pizza Hut and Domino's was less than 1 percent, with Domino's holding onto a 13.6 percent market share versus Pizza Hut's 14.3 percent. Pizza Hut was struggling due to lower popularity with younger consumers—who buy a larger proportion of pizzas—and was lagging in digital innovation.[8] "The pizza chain has stumbled to keep pace with its closest rivals," the article stated. Where Domino's and Papa John's receive at least 60 percent of their orders digitally, Pizza Hut's digital orders made up closer to "around 50 percent."[9] Additionally, Domino's and Papa John's had robust loyalty programs that incentivize customers to continue to order from them.[10] Pizza Hut did roll its own loyalty program out, but not until 2017.

In the second quarter, Domino's continued on its streak of strong same-store sales, with growth of 9.5 percent[11] to Pizza Hut's system sales growth of 2 percent.[12] The story in the third quarter wasn't much different, with Domino's seeing same-store sales growth of 8.4 percent[13] to Pizza Hut's 1 percent increase, reported *QSR*.[14] However, in the US, Pizza Hut's sales were down 4 percent.

Little changed in the fourth quarter, with Domino's achieving same-store sales growth of 4.2 percent, and 7.7 percent for the 2017 fiscal year as a whole (which didn't even include sales on New Year's Eve, since the company shifted its year-end date to December 31 instead of January 1).[15] Pizza Hut's US same-store sales rose 2 percent in the last quarter and 4.2 percent systemwide, reported *Ad Age*.[16] Despite the rise during the fourth quarter, it was not enough to pull Pizza Hut ahead. The fact is, Pizza Hut had been struggling, and would continue to struggle for a few more quarters.

With that year-end tally, Domino's claimed its win as the largest pizza chain (see Figure 2).

U.S. GROWTH CONTINUES TO BE BEST IN CLASS

Top 10 QSR Brands Average Same Store Sales
2010-Q3 2017

Source: Technomic Top 10 Public QSR companies
Comparable calendar quarters (SBUX)
Results: Company filings and Bloomberg

FIGURE 2

Beyond Sales

Although Domino's sales pulled it to the top of the pizza chain heap, it was also getting a lot of things right operationally, where other chains were struggling. Looking at data from Trefis,[17] which compared Domino's, Pizza Hut, and Papa John's, where Domino's saw retail sales growth rise from $10 billion in 2014 to $15.8 billion in 2018, Pizza Hut had effectively flat sales growth—from $12.1 billion to $12.2 billion between 2014 and 2018—and Papa John's held steady at $3.4 billion. In terms of sales growth, where Domino's saw a slight drop percentage-wise between 2017 and 2018, from 14.5 to 9.9 percent, Pizza Hut saw a 1.5 percent increase and Papa John's a 9.4 percent decline.

But operating margins are where Domino's truly shined in 2018, with 37.9 percent, up from 31.1 percent in 2017. Pizza Hut dropped from 38.2 percent to 35.2 percent in that same period, and Papa John's dropped from 8.5 to 1.9 percent. It turns out, innovation and investment in technology can provide a sustainable competitive advantage for a company that fortified its core product with a solid offering. Now that Domino's has reached the pinnacle of success, it will be harder to knock it far off its perch thanks to the investments it has made in its infrastructure.

"For Domino's Pizza, cracking the international code for success hasn't been as difficult as one might think for a pseudo-Italian food that is about as American as apple pie. Pizza is a surprisingly translatable meal around the world."

—*FORBES*

CHAPTER SEVENTEEN

THE INTER- NATIONAL OPPORTUNITY

Although Domino's roots are as a small-town, locally grown pizzeria chain, its aspirations are global, as evidenced by its rising number of non-US store locations. With demand for pizza higher in other countries than in the US, focusing resources internationally makes sense for most pizza chains.

The good news is that, according to the PMQ 2019 Pizza Power Report,[1] pizza shops are thriving internationally. Valued at just under $145 billion in total, the market's five-year forecasted growth rate is 10.7 percent worldwide, indicating plenty of upside potential for companies with the financial resources to pursue a bigger cut of that pie.

At Domino's, the average annual same-store growth was 5.6 percent between 1997 and 2018. Domestically, its same-store sales growth averaged 3.9 percent (see Figure 3).[2]

Domino's international expansion began in 1983, when its first location outside the US was opened in Winnipeg, Manitoba, Canada. Since then, the company has established

SAME STORE SALES TRACK RECORD

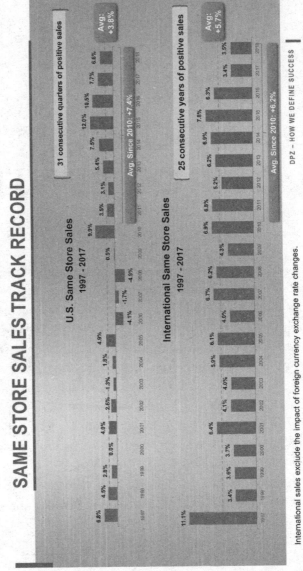

Internatioanal sales exclude the impact of foreign currency exchange rate changes.

FIGURE 3

more than ten thousand stores in more than ninety countries, not including the US.

Go Where the Growth Potential Is

International markets where demand for pizza is currently high include China, Italy, Russia, and Brazil. Many pizza chains have turned their attention to China, or did pre-coronavirus, because of its huge upside potential. PMQ China anticipated that Pizza Hut would open one thousand new units in China in 2019—many times more units than the fifty units each that Domino's and Papa John's planned to open—adding to its sizable 2,200-store base.[4]

Strong competition is dampening sales of pizza in Italy, with 50 percent of new pizzerias having closed their doors within five years of opening. This has been a trend since 2013, according to RistoNews. Those weathering the storm are doing so through innovation, developing newer dough and crust options and adding healthier topping options. While pizzas are popular in Russia, parbaked crusts are gaining serious momentum for consumers who want food that can be easily transported and has a longer shelf life. Parbaked has replaced fresh and even frozen dough as the most popular form of pizza there, reports Elena Shirokova in Moscow in PMQ's 2019 Pizza Power Report,[3] though pizza is viewed primarily as a fast-food option.

That perception is changing in Sweden, where pizza is going up-market, being served in higher-end restaurants and at resorts and pubs there. For that reason, there has been a rise in pizza competitions and baking events, Mikael Lundgren of Sveba-Dahlen reports.[4] A shift to healthier ingredients is also occurring in Brazil, where a surge of Italian immigrants in the early 1900s had already made pizza a menu mainstay. Today, pizza is gaining respect and heightened interest, thanks to chefs testing new baking techniques and toppings, Carlos Zoppetti of ConPizza says.[5]

American chains, while still expanding moderately in the US, continue to open stores more aggressively in international markets. Between 2017 and 2018, Domino's added 232 locations internationally, Pizza Hut opened 192 more units, and Papa John's opened 146 more global storefronts. Domino's presence is strongest in Australia and India, with locations in 88 more countries.

Domino's Global Vision for Domination

Domino's goal of building a base of 25,000 global stores by 2025 is within its reach, given it already has a base approaching 16,000 locations. Between 2012 and 2018, Domino's had net growth of 5,612 stores.[6]

Its revenue target for that milestone is $25 billion, with the company holding on to its #1 market position. And with non-US stores generating higher revenue growth, the company is smart to pay more attention to international markets. In fact, global retail sales growth has ranged from a low of 5.8 percent to a high of 9.2 percent since 2012, with US growth ranging from a low of 1.6 percent to a high of 6.6 percent. International growth has exceeded domestic sales growth consistently since 2012.

Retail Dive summarized Domino's plan for growth:

Domino's goals would lead to the pizza chain growing global sales twofold—its 2017 global retail sales were just over $12.2

billion—and add about 10,000 units. This would be a tall order for some QSR brands, but not Domino's, which already has the largest slice of the pizza industry. The company has been one of the only top pizza chains to consistently post same-store sales growth in the last few years, with Pizza Hut and Papa John's reporting declining sales, so it is definitely headed on a path toward world pizza domination.[7]

Fortressing as a Global Marketing Strategy

To combat competitive pressures and create a barrier to entry, Domino's has had great success with fortressing as a marketing strategy. That is, it is locating its new stores in such close proximity to its customers that orders are delivered faster and fresher than the competition or third-party delivery services could achieve. In many cases, such an approach involves reconfiguring delivery radiuses, rather than expanding the service area, so that there are more stores to deliver to the same customer base. In Las Vegas, for example, an area served by three Domino's stores was redesigned to be served by four. (The visual of such a process looks a lot like congressional redistricting based on population size.)

Although cannibalizing sales at existing locations is always a concern with the insertion of new stores in close proximity, Domino's locates its stores far enough apart that the improved customer service experience is enough to drive higher sales and attract more carryout business. The result is higher total sales for the stores in the area.

With fortressing, customers receive better service, delivery drivers travel shorter distances and can complete more deliveries in less time, carryout sales rise due to greater convenience, profitability is easier and more sustainable, and the barrier to entry for competitors is much higher. With Domino's excellent customer service and established loyalty, it is much more difficult for a new entrant to make much headway. Domino's demonstrated that in India, where one of its major competitors left the market after being unable to break through Domino's fortress. It simply couldn't be competitive, so it closed up shop.

In the UK, fortressing also proved successful. In Exeter, Domino's added a store, upping the total to three, and saw increased overall sales due to shorter delivery times. Sales between 2013 and 2018 were up 106.5 percent. The same result is evident in Nottingham, as well, where four new stores were added since 2013 and total sales for the area were up 76.8 percent between 2013 and 2018. The biggest reason behind the increase there is the average delivery time of 23.9 minutes—few competitors can best that time.

Both UK cities continue to achieve double-digit growth following the added storefronts. Exeter's average weekly unit sales were up 14.5 percent and Nottingham's were up 22.6 percent between 2015 and 2018. Long term, fortressing has proven useful in keeping competitors out and boosting loyalty to the Domino's brand.

International Competition

While US and international pizza chains are certainly all vying for the same customers, non-pizza restaurants and quick-serve outlets are also trying to muscle in on the market. "Uber Eats, GrubHub, and DoorDash are making it easier for other restaurants large and small to get in on the action, too," the Motley

Fool[8] stated. Overseas, Swiggy in India and Meituan in China are delivery service equivalents.

Although Domino's remains bullish on international growth, leveraging its market leader reputation in the delivery space, there is tremendous growth potential in food delivery, *Forbes* states, primarily because only 11 percent of the world's population currently has access to food delivery platforms. Accordingly, there is huge upside potential:[9]

> Online food delivery is set to supersize to a hefty $200 billion by 2025. . . . In 2018, Frost & Sullivan estimated the industry at $82 billion in terms of gross revenue bookings and is set to more than double by 2025, backed by a cumulative growth rate of 14 percent.[10]

If Domino's continues to focus on growing traffic and orders, rather than increasing order size, as it has been, odds are good it will achieve its goal.

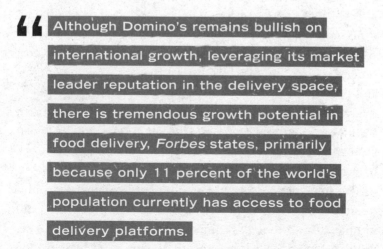

Although Domino's remains bullish on international growth, leveraging its market leader reputation in the delivery space, there is tremendous growth potential in food delivery, *Forbes* states, primarily because only 11 percent of the world's population currently has access to food delivery platforms.

Financial Performance

With international expansion fueling much of Domino's revenue growth, a look at Domino's stock performance may give a
sense of where the company has been and where it is headed.
The company went public in July 2004 on the New York Stock
Exchange as DPZ with an initial share price of $14.10. That
value quickly dropped the first day due to lack of interest, however. Over the next few years, the value rose slowly, hitting a
high of $33 in 2007 but then dropping to $3.03 in 2008, as the
Great Recession took hold and the housing market plummeted. That was the economy's and Domino's low point, with
improvements on the horizon.

As the stock price started to inch up, a video prank in 2009
drove the price down again slightly. Fortunately, that bad news
was quickly followed by some good—the complete overhaul of
Domino's lackluster pizza at the end of 2009. That campaign,
and a positive response to the new pizza's taste, drove the company's stock price up to $39 in 2012.

A series of smart decisions led the stock price to rise higher,
from removing the word "pizza" from its logo as the company
added sandwiches, chicken, and desserts to its menu to boost
order size, to technology investments that improved operations
and positioned the company as a cool tech company, rather
than a mature food service operation. In March 2016, following
a promising financial report and news that Domino's had been
dubbed a recognized leader in mobile technology, the stock
once again rose. By 2017, the stock price had hit $212.

The stock price continued to climb even after turnaround
master Patrick Doyle announced he would step down as CEO
in June 2018. Although it dipped slightly in 2018 to $173, be-
tween 2018 and 2020, it rose steadily. It closed at a high of $383

in April 2020 despite the coronavirus pandemic's restrictions. With carryout and delivery service deemed essential during shelter-in-place orders, Domino's appeared to be one of the industries to potentially benefit from closures in virtually all other industries. Families stuck at home could at least order pizza to restore some sense of normalcy.

Domino's stock price has appreciated 2,200 percent between 2010 and 2020 and it has the financial resources to weather the economic downturn caused by the global pandemic, suggests the Motley Fool. Certainly, the company's operational efficiencies, access to data and an ability to mine it for clues regarding needed changes or market moves, and a commitment to innovation have set it up for continued success in the next few years.

Domino's rise from pizzeria start-up to regional player to national brand and then global leader has many lessons to offer entrepreneurs and business owners. Founder Tom Monaghan infused the company with a work ethic and commitment to uncovering and applying best practices that serves the company well today, more than five decades after the opening of its first store.

One thing that Monaghan and Domino's has done well from the start is staying hyper-focused on its original product. Unlike other companies that branched out from their core competencies in search of growth, Domino's remains committed to being the best at baking and delivering pizzas. To that goal it has also added providing an enjoyable customer experience, which it has pursued through its ongoing investment in technology systems.

The company's decisions throughout its history provide a solid list of lessons learned that organizations can apply to their own operations. Some of the key takeaways include:

Be known for one thing. Whether that's a product or brand or benefit, go all in on one aspect of your business. For Domino's initially, that one thing was pizza delivery. Although pizzas were easily purchased, few local pizzerias were promising fast delivery. It was a convenience that quick-serve restaurants hadn't yet adopted *en masse*, which made it easier for Domino's to establish itself as the market leader for pizza delivery. It also earned the "first mover advantage" through that smart decision, which, in many industries, enables the first mover to capture a substantial share of the market.

Reinvest in the company, especially early on. Monaghan lived a very humble life during the early years of Domino's, and even after he and his wife were first married they lived in a mobile home to save money so that he could reinvest the vast majority of revenue back in the business. That habit continued as the company grew, keeping it on sure financial footing even during economic downturns.

Unlike companies that over-invest in real estate or office accoutrements, Domino's kept things simple. Monaghan would lease or buy hole-in-the-wall locations for his pizza shops, since the Domino's business model really only required space for baking and packing, rather than a cafeteria or dining room. Conserving cash made it possible for Monaghan to buy other pizzerias, invest in equipment as it became available, and test new concepts—such as the sit-down restaurant format that he later shuttered. By pouring money back into the company, rather than paying himself large sums, Monaghan created a culture of self-sufficiency that drove later business decisions within the company.

Know where your customers live. Domino's knows its customers, probably better than most, if not all, pizza chains. That has been a key strength since Day One, when serving hungry college students was its primary aim. Monaghan at one point claimed to know the dorm capacities at most of the US colleges and universities. That information was important to his business because dorms were where his best customers lived.

That data fueled Domino's expansion, which began by targeting other college towns and later went worldwide by population size, presumably. In fact, the importance of data has always been evident within Domino's. It has been and will likely always be a data-driven enterprise. That data informs its business decisions, reducing the opportunity for actions to be taken based on gut feel or hunch. Customer insights have made Domino's the powerhouse that it is.

Pay attention to efficiency opportunities. On top of being fiscally conservative, Monaghan was also enamored with efficiency. He doggedly pursued operational efficiencies, from setting up a commissary system, to designing equipment to speed the pizza baking process, to developing his own process for placing cheese on pizzas quickly.

The commissary system was genius, allowing Domino's to negotiate better purchase prices for raw materials based on its ability to buy in larger quantities, for several pizzerias. The commissary then supplied all of the local Domino's shops within a certain geographic radius. By holding materials at a central location, that also reduced the amount of storage space each retail shop required. Deliveries were made regularly, also ensuring ingredients were fresh.

Monaghan's investment in a "Big Red" oven—the world's largest pizza oven of its time—was one of the first examples of investing in manufacturing equipment that improved internal operations. The oven had a Ferris-wheel design, which provided a larger capacity—up to ninety pizzas could be baked simultaneously.

> " Monaghan's investment in a "Big Red" oven—the world's largest pizza oven of its time—was one of the first examples of investing in manufacturing equipment that improved internal operations. The oven had a Ferris-wheel design, which provided a larger capacity—up to ninety pizzas could be baked simultaneously.

But Monaghan knew that individuals could also improve processes through their own action. Through his experience in making pizzas, he developed his own "hand cheesing" technique that spread the perfect amount of cheese quickly and easily, and kept the pizza production process moving as efficiently as possible. By looking for opportunities to improve internal efficiency, Domino's has discovered ways to incrementally improve its operations on a consistent basis. Those efficiency improvements have undoubtedly improved its profitability.

Study your competition. When Monaghan was still developing the Domino's pizzeria concept, he visited three hundred rival pizzerias, tasting their products, examining their spaces, and studying their processes. He wanted to know what each did well and where they could improve so that he could cherry-pick the best practices for his company.

Gathering competitive intelligence is frequently what enables one company to progress faster than others, because it can identify current industry best practices and adopt them, to build a company and a culture that performs at an optimal level across the board. There's no way to do that, however, unless and until you study existing practices and assess what could be done better, if anything. Monaghan did that, for practically every aspect of the business.

Focus on traffic, not order size. Although many quick-service restaurants have been focusing on ticket size—meaning the average amount an order is worth—Domino's, instead, has focused on increasing its traffic and number of orders. That focus has helped it achieve double-digit growth over the last five years. "Unlike other QSR brands, which have posted continual declines in traffic growth, Domino's order growth was 7.4 percent in 2017 with ticket growth at 3.1 percent."[1] This approach is sound, since attracting more customer volume is likely to result in steady increases in sales.

Invest in technology. One of Domino's major strengths as a company has always been its heavy investment in technology. From the outset, the company understood the power that technology provided to enable fast growth and higher profitability. Investing in systems that captured and analyzed data made it possible to shift gears when necessary, in response to trends the data identified. Technology enabled Domino's to forge a closer relationship with its customers, due to the vast amounts of information the company collected about their orders, frequency of orders, preference for delivery or carryout, customer address, and other factors. That familiarity helped build loyalty that has helped the company become impervious to new competitors.

Retain control of systems that provide a proprietary advantage. Despite being the lone holdout adopting a popular point-of-sale (POS) system, Domino's understood the advantage of developing its POS system in-house. At the time, competitors scoffed at the investment of resources to that effort, choosing instead to modify off-the-shelf systems that could be rolled out quickly across their franchises. But by building its own Pulse system, Domino's maintained strict control of all of its customer and internal operating data.

Where other pizza companies left themselves vulnerable by allowing third-party technology firms access to their data, Domino's protected it. With 20/20 hindsight, many companies now laud that decision.

Modify only one variable at a time when initiating change. Domino's experience with its pizza recipe during the Great Recession is a great lesson about changing too many factors at once. During that time, when Domino's franchisees were looking for any way to reduce product costs and improve profitability, different groups worked on ways to lower costs of all of the ingredients. One group worked to reduce the cost of the dough by changing out some ingredients. Another worked on lowering the cost of the sauce, and another the cheese and the toppings. On their own, those changes were barely noticeable; however, when taken together, the resulting product was more of a Frankenpizza. And customers noticed.

When complaints started pouring in about the poor pizza taste, Domino's took a step back to evaluate its product and process and discovered what had happened. The pizza costs had been lowered, but customers were receiving a subpar pizza that was embarrassing to Domino's. The only solution was to start over from scratch. They approached it as an opportunity—an opportunity to create the best pizza ever. But the problem started by changing too many variables in the baking process simultaneously.

Avoid political or religious connections. Many companies have discovered too late how quickly customers will react when leaders publicly support a controversial cause or make a controversial statement. That situation was never more clear than in the late 1980s, though the same advice holds true today, in 2020.

Monaghan was well known as a devout Catholic, and was respected for the role that faith played in his life. But when his personal views spilled into his business, he created challenges that Domino's had difficulty overcoming. Monaghan's personal support of a statewide measure to block access to funding for abortions, and his resulting decision to cancel an event scheduled to occur at Domino's headquarters, drew the ire of the National Organization for Women (NOW), which called for a nationwide boycott of Domino's.

The sales decline hurt, so much so that Monaghan decided to sell the company in 1989 to distance himself from the controversy. Had he not taken such a public stand on a controversial topic, the whole situation could possibly have been averted.

Explore fortressing as a marketing strategy. One strategy that Domino's has clearly mastered internationally has been fortressing, or adding more locations to an area to improve customer satisfaction. The theory behind fortressing is that by providing superior customer service, you forge a relationship with customers that will be difficult for new competitors to overcome.

The downside, of course, is potential cannibalization of sales, or adding new locations to serve the same customer base. That only increases costs without increasing sales. That hasn't happened yet at Domino's, which is why the company continues to use it.

Domino's history isn't perfect and it has certainly had many missteps along the way, but the many things that it has done right are takeaways that other businesses can use to strengthen their operations.

ENDNOTES

Introduction

1. James Leonard, *Living the Faith: A Life of Tom Monaghan* (Ann Arbor: University of Michigan Press, 2012), p. 23.
2. James Leonard, *Living the Faith*, p. 23.

Chapter 1

1. "2020 Pizza Power Report," *PMQ Pizza Magazine*, December 2019. Accessed at https://www.pmq.com/pizza-power-report-2020/.
2. James Leonard, *Living the Faith*, p. 42.
3. Julie Sloane and Tom Monaghan, "Tom Monaghan Domino's Pizza THE PIONEERING PIZZA-DELIVERY CHAIN I STARTED ALMOST DIDN'T MAKE IT OUT OF THE OVEN," *Fortune Small Business*, September 1, 2003. Accessed at https://money.cnn.com/magazines/fsb/fsb_archive/2003/09/01/350799/.
4. James Leonard, *Living the Faith*, p. 54.

Chapter 2

1. James Leonard, *Living the Faith*, p. 54.
2. James Leonard, *Living the Faith*, p. 55.
3. Julie Sloane and Tom Monaghan, "Tom Monaghan Domino's Pizza . . ."
4. FundingUniverse report on Domino's Pizza. Accessed at http://www.fundinguniverse.com/company-histories/domino-s-inc-history/.

5. Thomas S. Dicke, *Franchising in America: The Development of a Business Method, 1840–1980* (Chapel Hill: University of North Carolina Press, 1992), p. 1.

6. Michael Seid, "The History of Franchising," The Balance Small Business, June 25, 2019. Accessed at https://www.thebalancesmb .com/the-history-of-franchising-1350455.

7. Jay Pederson, *International Directory of Company Histories*, Vol. 93 (St. James Press, 2008), p. 49. Accessed at https://books.google .com/books?id=N7EnAQAAIAAJ&q=Pizza+Hut+1966+145 +franchise+units&dq=Pizza+Hut+1966+145+franchise+units &hl=en&newbks=1&newbks_redir=0&sa=X&ved=2ahUKEwj T8IPS7uflAhUhuVkKHaZ0AYoQ6AEwAHoECAYQAg.

8. "A Brief History of McDonalds." Accessed at http://www.mc spotlight.org/company/company_history.html.

9. James Leonard, *Living the Faith*, page 59.

10. Julie Sloane and Tom Monaghan, "Tom Monaghan Domino's Pizza . . ."

11. Tom Monaghan and Robert Anderson, *Pizza Tiger* (New York: Random House, 1986), p. 110.

12. Tom Monaghan and Robert Anderson, *Pizza Tiger*, p. 110.

13. James Leonard, *Living the Faith*, p. 59.

14. James Leonard, *Living the Faith*, p. 62.

15. Tom Monaghan and Robert Anderson, *Pizza Tiger*, p. 112.

16. Tom Monaghan and Robert Anderson, *Pizza Tiger*, p. 112.

Chapter 3

1. Tom Monaghan and Robert Anderson, *Pizza Tiger*, p. 113.

2. John McDonough and Karen Egolf, eds., *The Advertising Age Encyclopedia of Advertising* (New York: Routledge, 2015), p. 1356.

3. Tom Monaghan and Robert Anderson, *Pizza Tiger*, p. 114.

4. Tom Monaghan and Robert Anderson, *Pizza Tiger*, p. 115.

5. James Leonard, *Living the Faith*, p. 65.

6. Tom Monaghan and Robert Anderson, *Pizza Tiger*, p. 128.

7. Company Histories. Accessed at https://www.company-histories .com/Dominos-Inc-Company-History.html.

8. James Leonard, *Living the Faith*, p. 69.

9. Tom Monaghan and Robert Anderson, *Pizza Tiger*, p. 128.

10. James Leonard, *Living the Faith*, p. 67.

11. *Amstar Corp. vs. Domino's Pizza, Inc.*, 1980, via Leagle. Accessed at https://www.leagle.com/decision/1980867615f2d2521829.

12. Tom Monaghan and Robert Anderson, *Pizza Tiger*, p. 137.

13. Tom Monaghan and Robert Anderson, *Pizza Tiger*, p. 138.

Chapter 4

1. Thomas Durso, "Sports of the Times; Pizza King and His Tigers," *New York Times*, June 6, 1984. Accessed at https://www.nytimes.com/1984/06/06/sports/sports-of-the-times-pizza-king-and-his-tigers.html.

2. Jean Halliday, "Variety Is the Spice of Life in Domino's Pizza," *Crain's Detroit Business*, August 2, 1993.

3. Jim Osterman, "Domino's Great Delivery Deal: The Pizza's There in 30 Minutes or It's $3 Cheaper," *Adweek*, August 8, 1987.

4. Dan Gentile, "The Historical Timeline of the McDonald's Menu," Thrillist.com, January, 4, 2014. Accessed at https://www.thrillist.com/eat/nation/a-historical-timeline-of-everything-on-the-mcdonald-s-menu-thrillist-nation.

5. James Leonard, *Living the Faith*, p. 164.

6. Associated Press, "Domino's Announces 30 Slice Pizza," April 28, 1993.

7. Zoe Bain, "Domino's Vegan Pizza—Soy Cheese Pizza," *Delish*, July 17, 2015. Accessed at https://www.delish.com/food/news/a39567/dominos-vegan-pizza/.

8. Your Dictionary biography, Tom Monaghan. Accessed at https://biography.yourdictionary.com/tom-monaghan.

9. Thomas S. Dicke, *Franchising in America*, p. 133.

10 Thomas S. Dicke, *Franchising in America*, p. 133.

11. Reference for Business, Domino's Pizza, Inc. Accessed at https://www.referenceforbusiness.com/history2/60/Domino-s-Pizza-Inc.html.

12. Hitt, Ireland, and Hoskisson, *Strategic Management Cases: Competitiveness and Globalization* (Mason, OH: South-Western, Cengage Publishing, 2013), p. 101.

13. Tom Monaghan and Robert Anderson, *Pizza Tiger*, p. 269.

14. Tom Monaghan and Robert Anderson, *Pizza Tiger*, pp. 269–270.

15. Chris Kelsch, "Marco's Pizza," Supply Chain Best Practices, October 26, 2017. Accessed at https://www.bestsupplychainpractices.com/2017/10/marco-s-pizza/.

16. Hitt, Ireland, and Hoskisson, *Strategic Management Cases*, p. 102.

17. "Domino's Inc. History," Funding Universe profile. Accessed at http://www.fundinguniverse.com/company-histories/domino-s-inc-history/.

18. Tom Peters, "Going for the Gold in Dough." Accessed at https://tompeters.com/columns/going-for-the-gold-in-dough/.

19. Tom Monaghan, "The Importance of Focus," *Legatus Magazine*, May 1, 2010. Accessed at https://legatus.org/the-importance-of-focus/.

Chapter 5

1. Pizza Hall of Fame, "Domino's Pizza." Accessed at http://pizzahalloffame.com/dominos-pizza/.

2. Matt Blitz, "Who Delivered the First Pizza?" *Food & Wine*, March 29, 2016. Accessed at https://www.foodandwine.com/news/political-story-first-pizza-delivery.

3. Emelyn Rude, "What Take-Out Food Can Teach You about American History," *Time*, April 14, 2016. Accessed at https://time.com/4291197/take-out-delivery-food-history/.

4. Funding Universe profile of Domino's Pizza, Inc.

5. Tim McIntyre, phone interview, August 12, 2019.

6. Julie Sloane and Tom Monaghan, "Tom Monaghan Domino's Pizza . . ."

7. Andrew F. Smith, *Food and Drink in American History: A "Full Course" Encyclopedia*, Vol. 1 (Santa Barbara, CA: ABC-CLIO, 2013), p. 679.

8. Gary Allen and Ken Albala, *The Business of Food: Encyclopedia of the Food and Drink Industries* (Westport, CT: Greenwood Press, 2007), p. 127.

9. James Leonard, *Living the Faith*, p. 45.

10. James Leonard, *Living the Faith*, p. 125.

11. Don Daszkowski, "Domino's Pizza Founder Tom Monaghan Biography," The Balance Small Business, November 26, 2019. Accessed at https://www.thebalancesmb.com/tom-monaghan-biography-1350964.

12. Scott Weiner, "Scott's Pizza Chronicles: A Brief History of the Pizza Box," Serious Eats, July 8, 2011. Accessed at https://slice .seriouseats.com/2011/07/a-brief-history-of-the-pizza-box.html.

13. "HotBags . . . Turning up the heat on delivery and hotbag manufacturers," *PMQ Pizza Magazine*, January 2002. Accessed at https://www.pmq.com/hotbags-turning-up-the-heat-on-delivery -and-hotbag-manufacturers/.

14. Domino's website. Accessed at https://www.dominos.com/en /about-pizza/.

Chapter 6

1. Tom Monaghan, "Growth Strategies: Tom Monaghan," *Entrepreneur*, October 10, 2008. Accessed at https://www.entrepreneur .com/article/197674.

2. James Evans, *Quality & Performance Excellence: Management, Organization, and Strategy*, 8th ed. (Boston: Cengage Learning, 2017), p. 215.

3. Video interview for Sports Faith International, March 10, 2010. Accessed at https://www.youtube.com/watch?v=EoS2bTp91-c.

4. "Domino's Inc. History," Funding Universe profile.

5. Associated Press, "Domino's Puts the Brakes on 30-Minute Deliveries," December 22, 1993. Accessed at https://www.deseret .com/1993/12/22/19083018/domino-s-puts-the-brakes-on -30-minute-deliveries.

6. Michael Janofsky, "Domino's Ends Fast-Pizza Pledge after Big Award to Crash Victim," *New York Times*, December 22, 1993. Accessed at https://www.nytimes.com/1993/12/22/business /domino-s-ends-fast-pizza-pledge-after-big-award-to-crash -victim.html.

7. Michael Janofsky, "Domino's Ends Fast-Pizza Pledge after Big Award to Crash Victim."

8. Zachary Crockett, "How Domino's Pizza Lost Its Mascot," Priceonomics, July 8, 2014. Accessed at https://priceonomics.com /how-dominos-pizza-lost-its-mascot/.

9. John Brownlee, "Death and Pizza: How Domino's Lost Its Mascot," *Fast Company*, July 10, 2014. Accessed at https://www.fast company.com/3032911/kidnapping-death-pizza-how-dominos -lost-its-mascot.

10. Michael Janofsky, "Domino's Ends Fast-Pizza Pledge after Big Award to Crash Victim."

Chapter 7

1. Tom Monaghan, "A Pizza Mogul Gets His Priorities Straight," *National Catholic Register*, October 12, 1997. Accessed at https://www.ncregister.com/site/article/a_pizza_mogul_gets_his_priorities_straight.

2. Tom Monaghan, "A Pizza Mogul Gets His Priorities Straight."

3. Ted Sylvester, "With or without Tom—Domino's Boycott Continues," *Agenda*, November 1989. Accessed at https://aadl.org/node/246534.

4. Peter Boyer, "The Deliverer: A Pizza Mogul Funds a Moral Crusade," *New Yorker*, February 19, 2007. Accessed at https://www.newyorker.com/magazine/2007/02/19/the-deliverer.

5. Ted Sylvester, "With or without Tom—Domino's Boycott Continues."

6. Ted Sylvester, "With or without Tom—Domino's Boycott Continues."

7. Ted Sylvester, "With or without Tom—Domino's Boycott Continues."

8. Tom Monaghan, "A Pizza Mogul Gets His Priorities Straight."

9. Tom Monaghan, "Growth Strategies: Tom Monaghan."

10. Eben Shapiro, "Domino's Chief Open to a Sale," *New York Times*, September 12, 1989. Accessed at https://www.nytimes.com/1989/09/12/business/domino-s-chief-open-to-a-sale.html.

11. Reuters, "Domino's Pizza Suitors Cited," *New York Times*, May 26, 1990. Accessed at https://www.nytimes.com/1990/05/26/business/company-news-domino-s-pizza-suitors-cited.html.

12. Associated Press, "Domino's to Trim Jobs and Benefits," *New York Times*, November 2, 1989. Accessed at https://www.nytimes.com/1989/11/02/business/company-news-domino-s-to-trim-jobs-and-benefits.html.

13. Eben Shapiro, " Domino's Chief Open to a Sale."

14. Doron Levin, "Domino Founder Seizes Command," *New York Times*, December 12, 1991. Accessed at https://www.nytimes.com/1991/12/10/business/domino-founder-seizes-command.html.

15. Doron Levin, "Domino Founder Seizes Command."

16. Doron Levin, "Domino Founder Seizes Command."

17. Doron Levin, "Stock Sale Is Planned at Domino's," *New York Times*, February 28, 1992. Accessed at https://www.nytimes.com /1992/02/28/business/company-news-stock-sale-is-planned-at -domino-s.html.

18. Associated Press, "Plans Sale of Domino's Pizza, Baseball Team," February 28, 1992. Accessed at https://apnews.com/81929239f 20f5fda7d648cf9552b3600.

19. James Leonard, *Living the Faith*, p. 147.

20. James Leonard, *Living the Faith*, p. 150.

21. Julie Sloane and Tom Monaghan, "Tom Monaghan Domino's Pizza . . ."

22. James Leonard, *Living the Faith*, p. 152.

23. James Leonard, *Living the Faith*, p. 169.

24. James Leonard, *Living the Faith*, p. 169.

25. James Leonard, *Living the Faith*, p. 170.

26. Lauren Rae Silva, "Domino's Buys Back Shares from Bain," TheStreet, March 13, 2006. Accessed at https://www.thestreet .com/investing/stocks/dominos-buys-back-shares-from-bain -10273265.

27. James Leonard, *Living the Faith*, p. 195.

Chapter 8

1. Bernice Kanner, "Pizza Wars," *New York* magazine, September 1, 1987. Accessed at https://books.google.com/books?id=l -UCAAAAMBAJ&pg=PA20&dq=Little+Caesars+pizza+1987 +delivery+market&hl=en&sa=X&ved=2ahUKEwiPicXJzq3k AhWOzlkKHW78CUEQuwUwAXoECAEQBA#v=onepage &q=Little%20Caesars%20pizza%201987%20delivery%20 market&f=false.

2. Reference for Business: Papa John's. Accessed at https:// www.referenceforbusiness.com/history/Oe-Pa/Papa-John-s -International-Inc.html.

3. Steven Phillips, "Pizza's Home-Delivery War," *New York Times*, September 27, 1986. Accessed at https://www.nytimes.com /1986/09/27/business/pizza-s-home-delivery-war.html.

4. Company News, "Menu's Hot Item: Home Delivery," *New York Times*, September 5, 1988. Accessed at https://www.nytimes .com/1988/09/05/business/company-news-menus-hot-item -home-delivery.html.

5. Bernice Kanner, "Pizza Wars."

6. Nancy Ryan, "Domino's Must Change Its Ways Fast or Risk Losing Pizza War, Analysts Warn," *New York Daily News*, May 17, 1992. Accessed at https://www.nydailynews.com/bs-xpm-1992-05-17 -1992138089-story.html.

7. Steven Phillips, "Pizza's Home-Delivery War."

8. Steven Phillips, "Pizza's Home-Delivery War."

9. James Risen, "Prince of Pizza: Domino's Top Man Lives Out His Fantasies," *Los Angeles Times*, October 11, 1987. Accessed at https://www.latimes.com/archives/la-xpm-1987-10-11-fi-13386 -story.html.

10. Company News, "Menu's Hot Item: Home Delivery."

11. Nancy Ryan, "Domino's Must Change Its Ways Fast or Risk Losing Pizza War, Analysts Warn."

12. Company News, "Menu's Hot Item: Home Delivery."

13. Donald Nauss, "Pizza's Humble Giant Reaches for a Bigger Slice," *Los Angeles Times*, September 3, 1995. Accessed at https:// www.latimes.com/archives/la-xpm-1995-09-03-fi-41725-story .html.

14. "Domino's Inc. History," Funding Universe profile.

15. "Domino's Inc. History," Funding Universe profile.

16. Carol Tice, "How Little Caesar's Lost the Pizza Wars," CBS News, December 1, 2010. Accessed at https://www.cbsnews.com/news /how-little-caesars-lost-the-pizza-wars/.

17. "Little Caesars," Encyclopedia.com. Accessed at https://www .encyclopedia.com/marketing/encyclopedias-almanacs -transcripts-and-maps/little-caesar-enterprises-inc.

18. Catherine Clifford, "Papa John's Founder: 'I Am the American Dream,'" *Entrepreneur* magazine, June 20, 2014. Accessed at https://www.entrepreneur.com/article/235040.

19. "Papa John's Inc. History," Funding Universe profile. Accessed at http://www.fundinguniverse.com/company-histories/papa -john-s-international-inc-history/).

20. "Papa John's," Encyclopedia.com. Accessed at https://www
.encyclopedia.com/social-sciences-and-law/economics-business
-and-labor/businesses-and-occupations/papa-johns.
21. John Greenwald, "Slice, Dice, and Devour," *Time*, October 26,
1998. Accessed at http://content.time.com/time/subscriber
/article/0,33009,989415,00.html.
22. Catherine Clifford, "Papa John's Founder: 'I Am the American
Dream.'"
23. Drake Baer, "This Marketing Insight Made Papa John's a
Household Name," *Business Insider*, May 21, 2014. Accessed at
https://www.businessinsider.com/papa-johns-marketing-
insight-2014-5?IR=T/.
24. "Papa John's Inc. History," Funding Universe profile.
25. "Papa John's Inc. History," Funding Universe profile.
26. John Greenwald, "Slice, Dice, and Devour."

Chapter 9

1. "Growing Pizza Chain Has Latino Flavor," *Los Angeles Times*, July
23, 1991. Accessed at https://www.latimes.com/archives/la-xpm
-1991-07-23-fi-134-story.html.
2. Donald Nauss, "Pizza's Humble Giant Reaches for a Bigger Slice."
3. Donald Nauss, "Pizza's Humble Giant Reaches for a Bigger Slice."
4. Donald Nauss, "Pizza's Humble Giant Reaches for a Bigger Slice."
5. Associated Press, "Little Caesar's Pizza Chain Will Jump on the
Delivery Train," *Los Angeles Times*, June 13, 1995. Accessed at
https://www.latimes.com/archives/la-xpm-1995-06-13-fi-12788
-story.html.
6. Associated Press, "Little Caesar's Pizza Chain Will Jump on the
Delivery Train."
7. Associated Press, "Pizza Hut's Commercial Falls Flat with Domino's," January 11, 1991. Accessed at https://www.latimes.com
/archives/la-xpm-1991-01-11-fi-8105-story.html.
8. Stuart Elliott, "The Hut Turns Up the Heat in the War of Pizza
Chains," *New York Times*, December 23, 1991. Accessed at
https://www.nytimes.com/1991/12/23/business/media
-business-advertising-hut-turns-up-heat-war-pizza-chains.html.

9. Greg Johnson, "Pizza Maker Reaches for Its Slice," *Los Angeles Times,* October 29, 1998. Accessed at https://www.latimes.com/archives/la-xpm-1998-oct-29-fi-37032-story.html.

10. Greg Johnson, "Pizza Maker Reaches for Its Slice."

11. Richard Gibson, "Popular Pizza Chain Tries a New Gimmick—Taste," *Wall Street Journal,* April 28, 1997. Accessed at https://www.wsj.com/articles/SB862173849227647000.

12. Alexei Barrionuevo, "Price War! Price War!: Pizza Chains Follow Burger Joints' Lead with New Deals," *Los Angeles Times,* April 29, 1993. Accessed at https://www.latimes.com/archives/la-xpm-1993-04-29-fi-28409-story.html.

13. Alexei Barrionuevo, "Price War! Price War!"

14. Alexei Barrionuevo, "Price War! Price War!"

15. Roberto Ferdman, "The Chipotle Effect: Why America Is Obsessed with Fast Casual Food," *Washington Post,* February 2, 2015.

16. "Who Will Be the Chipotle of the Pizza Industry," July 28, 2011. Accessed at https://www.pizzamarketplace.com/articles/who-will-be-the-chipotle-of-the-pizza-industry/.

Chapter 10

1. Amy Jacques, "Domino's Delivers during Crisis," *Public Relations Strategist,* PRSA, August 17, 2009. Accessed at https://apps.prsa.org/Intelligence/TheStrategist/Articles/view/8226/102/Domino_s_Delivers_During_Crisis_The_Company_s_Step #.XpIIr4hKiUk_.

2. Raymund Flandez, "Domino's Response Offers Lessons in Crisis Management," *Wall Street Journal,* April 20, 2009. Accessed at https://blogs.wsj.com/independentstreet/2009/04/20/dominos-response-offers-lessons-in-crisis-management/.

3. Richard Gibson, "A Smaller Slice of the Pie," *Wall Street Journal,* February 23, 2009. Accessed at https://www.wsj.com/articles/SB123498018052714211.

4. Nelson Schwartz, "The Economy Looks a Lot Like Pizza," *New York Times,* January 6, 2008. Accessed at https://www.nytimes.com/2008/01/06/business/06maker.html.

5. Richard Gibson, "A Smaller Slice of the Pie."

6. Benny Evangelista, "How Domino's Responded to Prank Video," *San Francisco Chronicle*, May 3, 2009. Accessed at https://www .sfgate.com/business/article/How-Domino-s-responded-to -prank-video-3163363.php.

7. Stephanie Clifford, "Video Prank at Domino's Taints Brand," *New York Times*, April 15, 2009. Accessed at https://www .nytimes.com/2009/04/16/business/media/16dominos.html.

8. Benny Evangelista, "How Domino's Responded to Prank Video."

9. Raymund Flandez, "Domino's Response Offers Lessons in Crisis Management."

10. Benny Evangelista, "How Domino's Responded to Prank Video."

11. Amy Jacques, "Domino's Delivers during Crisis."

12. Amy Jacques, "Domino's Delivers during Crisis."

13. Stephanie Clifford, "Video Prank at Domino's Taints Brand."

14. Benny Evangelista, "How Domino's Responded to Prank Video."

15. Amy Jacques, "Domino's Delivers during Crisis."

16. Stephanie Clifford, "Video Prank at Domino's Taints Brand."

17. Richard Gibson, "A Smaller Slice of the Pie," *Wall Street Journal*, February 23, 2009.

18. Benny Evangelista, "How Domino's Responded to Prank Video."

19. Sarah Newell Williamson, "Domino's Pizza Gross-Out Prankster Pleads Guilty," *Charlotte Observer*, November 20, 2010. Accessed at https://www.charlotteobserver.com/latest-news/article9048248 .html_.

Chapter 11

1. "Who's Who: Dave Brandon," Pizza Marketplace, February 21, 2002. Accessed at https://www.pizzamarketplace.com/news /whos-who-dave-brandon/.

2. Suzanne Kapner, "Toys 'R Us Names IPO Veteran David Brandon as Its Next CEO," *Wall Street Journal*, June 2, 2015. Accessed at https://www.wsj.com/articles/toys-r-us-names-david-brandon -as-its-next-ceo-1433257729.

3. "Who's Who: Dave Brandon."

4. Erin White, "To Keep Its Employees, Domino's Decides It's Not All About Pay," *Wall Street Journal*, February 18, 2005. Accessed at https://www.post-gazette.com/business/businessnews/2005

/02/18/To-keep-employees-Domino-s-decides-it-s-not-all
-about-pay/stories/200502180276.

5. Erin White, "To Keep Its Employees, Domino's Decides It's Not all About Pay."

6. Erin White, "To Keep Its Employees, Domino's Decides It's Not all About Pay."

7. Daniel Denison, Robert Hooijberg, Nancy Lane, and Colleen Lief, *Leading Culture Change in Global Organizations: Aligning Culture and Strategy* (New York: John Wiley & Sons, 2012).

8. "How Domino's Pizza Drove 90x Increase in Stock Value by Acting Like a Tech Startup," *ProductHabits Blog.* Accessed at https://producthabits.com/dominos-pizza-drove-90x-increase-stock-value-acting-like-tech-startup/.

9. Kate Macarthur, "Marketing Malaise Hurts Domino's," *Ad Age*, October 1, 2008. Accessed at https://adage.com/article/news/marketing-malaise-hurts-domino-s/100108.

10. "Domino's to Offer $4 Pizza Value Meal," *Nation's Restaurant News*, March 28, 2008. Accessed at https://www.nrn.com/archive/dominos-offer-4-pizza-value-meal.

11. Patrick Dunn, "Patrick Doyle Led Domino's Daring Turnaround. Now He's Taking the Pizza Maker Online," *Ann Arbor Observer*, May 2016. Accessed at https://annarborobserver.com/articles/new_and_inspired.html#.XpOvcYhKiUk.

12. Company Histories. Accessed at https://www.company-histories.com/Dominos-Inc-Company-History.html.

13. Susan Burfield, "Domino's Atoned for Its Crimes against Pizza and Built a $9 Billion Empire," *Bloomberg Businessweek*, March 15, 2017. Accessed at https://www.bloomberg.com/features/2017-dominos-pizza-empire/.

14. Sam Ochs, "The Many Acts of Domino's Pizza," *QSR*, August 2010. Accessed at https://www.qsrmagazine.com/menu-innovations/many-acts-domino-s-pizza.

Chapter 12

1. Stephen Moore, "How Pizza Became a Growth Stock," *Wall Street Journal*, March 13, 2015. Accessed at https://www.wsj.com/articles/the-weekend-interview-with-j-patrick-doyle-how-pizza-became-a-growth-stock-1426286353.

2. Bret Thorn, "Patrick Doyle Leaves Legacy of Success at Domino's," *Nation's Restaurant News*, January 12, 2018. Accessed at https://www.nrn.com/people/patrick-doyle-leaves-legacy-success-domino-s.

3. Sarah Lockyer, "Patrick Doyle to Be Named Domino's CEO," *Nation's Restaurant News*, January 5, 2009. Accessed at https://www.nrn.com/archive/patrick-doyle-be-named-domino-s-ceo.

4. Michael Mink, "Patrick Doyle Dove into the Hot Kitchen to Make Domino's Pizza an Extra Large Success," *Investor's Business Daily*, September 14, 2018. Accessed at https://www.investors.com/news/management/leaders-and-success/patrick-doyle-dove-into-the-hot-kitchen-to-make-dominos-pizza-an-extra-large-success/.

5. Daniel Smith, "The Fall of Pizza," *QSR*, February 2011. Accessed at https://www.qsrmagazine.com/growth/fall-pizza?page=2.

6. "Consumers Are Expanding Their Definition of Fast Food, Reports Technomic," January 12, 2010. Accessed at https://www.businesswire.com/news/home/20100112006249/en/Consumers-Expanding-Definition-Fast-Food-Reports-Technomic.

7. Bret Thorn, "Patrick Doyle Leaves Legacy of Success at Domino's."

8. Carol Tice, "How Pizza Hut Got Its Groove Back," CBS News, April 19, 2010. Accessed at https://www.cbsnews.com/news/how-pizza-hut-got-its-groove-back/.

9. Bret Thorn, "2009 Year in Review," *Nation's Restaurant News*, December 21, 2009. Accessed at https://www.nrn.com/archive/2009-year-review.

10. Bret Thorn, "Patrick Doyle Leaves Legacy of Success at Domino's."

11. "Domino's Changing Its Pizza Recipe," *Los Angeles Times*, December 27, 2009. Accessed at https://www.latimes.com/archives/la-xpm-2009-dec-27-la-fi-consumerbriefs27-2009dec27-story.html.

12. Eric Cassano, "How Patrick Doyle Faced the Reality of Not Being the Best—and Took Steps to Put Domino's Back on Top," *Smart Business*, September 1, 2011. Accessed at https://www.sbnonline.com/article/how-patrick-doyle-faced-the-reality-of-not-being-the-best-and-took-steps-to-put-dominos-back-on-top/2/.

13. "Domino's CEO J. Patrick Doyle to Leave Company," *QSR* January 10, 2018. Accessed at https://www.qsrmagazine.com/news/dominos-ceo-j-patrick-doyle-leave-company.

14. Dale Buss, "As the Man Who Put Domino's in Motion, Patrick Doyle Wants to Keep the Momentum Going," *Forbes*, July 24, 2017. Accessed at https://www.forbes.com/sites/dalebuss/2017 /07/24/as-the-man-who-put-dominos-in-motion-patrick-doyle -wants-to-keep-the-momentum-going/#6572a6dc5735.

15. Dale Buss, "As the Man Who Put Domino's in Motion, Patrick Doyle Wants to Keep the Momentum Going."

16. Dale Buss, "Rising to the Top," *DBusiness*, March 27, 2018. Accessed at https://www.dbusiness.com/business-features/rising -to-the-top/.

17. Dale Buss, "Rising to the Top."

Chapter 13

1. Sam Ochs, "The Many Acts of Domino's Pizza."

2. Cynthia Than, "Domino's Admitted Their Pizza Tastes Like Cardboard and Won Back Our Trust," March 31, 2017. Accessed at https://www.inc.com/cynthia-than/dominos-admitted-their -pizza-tastes-like-cardboard-and-won-back-our-trust.html.

3. T. L. Stanley, "Russell Weiner, Domino's," *Adweek*, September 13, 2010. Accessed at https://www.adweek.com/brand-marketing /russell-weiner-dominos-94411/.

4. Jeff Beer, "How Domino's Became a Tech Company," *Fast Company*, May 22, 2014. Accessed at https://www.fastcompany.com /3030869/how-dominos-became-a-tech-company.

5. Eric Cassano, "How Patrick Doyle Faced the Reality of Not Being the Best—and Took Steps to Put Domino's Back on Top."

6. Phone interview with Russell Weiner, August 2019.

7. Nathan Bomey, "Ann Arbor's Domino's Pizza Changes Core Pizza Recipe," *Ann Arbor News*, December 16, 2009. Accessed at http://www.annarbor.com/business-review/dominos-pizza -fundamentally-altering-core-pizza-recipe/.

8. Russell Weiner, presentation to the University of Michigan Center for Entrepreneurship, December 8, 2015. Accessed at https://www.youtube.com/watch?v=mFTQFEyylMI&t=228s.

9. Eric Cassano, "How Patrick Doyle Faced the Reality of Not Being the Best—and Took Steps to Put Domino's Back on Top."

10. Nathan Bomey, "Ann Arbor's Domino's Pizza Changes Core Pizza Recipe."

11. Nathan Bomey, "Ann Arbor's Domino's Pizza Changes Core Pizza Recipe."

12. Eric Cassano, "How Patrick Doyle Faced the Reality of Not Being the Best—and Took Steps to Put Domino's Back on Top."

13. "Domino's Launches Massive $75 Million Ad Blitz," *Forbes*, December 22, 2009. Accessed at https://www.forbes.com/2009/12/21/dominos-pizza-recipe-ad-campaign-cmo-network-dominos.html#45fc5b1129a7.

14. Paul Farhi, "Behind Domino's Mea Culpa Ad Campaign," *Washington Post*, January 13, 2010. Accessed at https://www.washingtonpost.com/wp-dyn/content/article/2010/01/12/AR2010011201696.html.

15. Phone interview with Russell Weiner, August 2019.

16. Adrian Campos, "Why Domino's Spent Millions to Fix Its Pizza," Motley Fool, November 20, 2013. Accessed at https://www.fool.com/investing/general/2013/11/20/why-dominos-spent-millions-to-fix-its-pizza.aspx.

17. Susan Berfield, "Domino's Atoned for Its Crimes against Pizza and Built a $9 Billion Empire."

18. Nathan Bomey, "Domino's Turns Two Years of Recipe Research into Successful Product Overhaul," *Ann Arbor News*, November 5, 2010. Accessed at http://www.annarbor.com/business-review/dominos-pizza-formulas-remade-from-crust-to-cheese/.

19. Russell Weiner, presentation to the University of Michigan Center for Entrepreneurship, December 8, 2015.

20. Sean Gregory, "Domino's New Recipe: (Brutal) Truth in Advertising," *Time*, May 5, 2011. Accessed at http://content.time.com/time/business/article/0,8599,2069766-1,00.html.

Chapter 14

1. Domino's investor presentation, August 2019. Accessed at https://dominos.gcs-web.com/static-files/02f48705-3ae0-40c7-ad2c-52d812ae3cab.

2. Domino's press release, August 20, 2019. Accessed at https://www.prnewswire.com/news-releases/dominos-to-open-new-workspace-dedicated-to-collaborative-innovation-300903821.html.

3. Jonathan Maze, "Five Lessons from Domino's Comeback," *Restaurant Business*, January 18, 2018. Accessed at https://www

.restaurantbusinessonline.com/financing/five-lessons-dominos
-comeback.

4. Jonathan Maze, "How Domino's Became a Tech Company," *Nation's Restaurant News*, March 29, 2016. Accessed at https://www
.nrn.com/technology/how-domino-s-became-tech-company.

5. Suman Bhattacharyya, "Domino's In-House Technology Push Has Helped Increase Online Orders," DigiDay, October 17, 2018. Accessed at https://digiday.com/retail/dominos-house
-technology-push-helped-increase-online-orders/.

6. Bill Heitzeg presentation at CodeMash. Accessed at https://
www.infoq.com/presentations/Free-Pizza-A-Glimpse-Inside
-eCommerce-at-Domino-s-Pizza/.

7. Shareen Pathak, "Domino's Is Now 'An E-Commerce Company That Sells Pizza,'" DigiDay, April 3, 2015. Accessed at https://
digiday.com/marketing/dominos-now-e-commerce-company
-sells-pizza/.

8. "Domino's Pizza Tracker Nets One Millionth User," *QSR*, March 19, 2008. Accessed at https://www.qsrmagazine.com/news
/dominos-pizza-tracker-nets-one-millionth-user.

9. Brian Morrissey, "Form + Function," *Adweek*, April 10, 2008. Accessed at https://www.adweek.com/digital/form-function
-95163/.

10. Brian Morrissey, "Form + Function."

11. https://shortyawards.com/8th/dominos-anyware.

12. Emily Bryson York, "Why Pizza Giants Want Customers to Click, Not Call," *Ad Age*, April 20, 2009. Accessed at https://adage
.com/article/digital/pizza-giants-customers-click-call-delivery
/136087.

13. Alicia Kelso, "How Becoming 'A Tech Company That Sells Pizza' Delivered Huge for Domino's," *Forbes*, April 30, 2018. Accessed at https://www.forbes.com/sites/aliciakelso/2018/04/30/delivery
-digital-provide-dominos-with-game-changing-advantages
/#40767aa37771.

14. NPD custom research conducted for Domino's, June 2012, as reported in investor presentation. Accessed at http://media
.corporate-ir.net/media_files/IROL/13/135383/Domino
%27s%20Pizza%20Investor%20Day%20Presentation%20
for%20Thomson.pdf.

15. Kyle Wong, "How Domino's Transformed into an E-Commerce Powerhouse Whose Product Is Pizza," *Forbes*, January 2, 2018. Accessed at https://www.forbes.com/sites/kylewong/2018/01/26/how-dominos-transformed-into-an-ecommerce-powerhouse-whose-product-is-pizza/#749d6ccb7f76.

16. Kyle Wong, "How Domino's Transformed into an E-Commerce Powerhouse Whose Product Is Pizza."

17. Phone interview with Ritch Allison, August 2019.

18. Shareen Pathak, "Domino's Is Now 'An E-Commerce Company That Sells Pizza.'"

19. David Gianastasio, "Domino's Just Unveiled a Radical Pizza Delivery Car That Took 4 Years to Build," *Adweek*, October 22, 2015. Accessed at https://www.adweek.com/creativity/dominos-just-unveiled-radical-pizza-delivery-car-took-4-years-build-167707/.

20. Michael Martinez, "Domino's, Ford Test Consumer Appetite for Driverless Delivery," *Crain's Detroit Business*, August 29, 2017. Accessed at https://www.crainsdetroit.com/article/20170829/news/637606/dominos-ford-test-consumer-appetite-for-driverless-delivery.

21. Ritch Allison, phone interview, 2019.

22. Lizzy Alfs, "What's Next for Domino's Pizza? CEO Patrick Doyle Outlines Some Goals," *Ann Arbor News*, September 1, 2013. Accessed at http://www.annarbor.com/business-review/whats-next-for-dominos-pizza-ceo-patrick-doyle-outlines-some-goals/.

23. Alex Samuely, "Domino's Strong Mobile Sales Prove Millennials' Dependency on Digital Ordering," Retail Dive, approx. 2015. Accessed at https://www.retaildive.com/ex/mobilecommerce daily/dominos-strong-mobile-sales-prove-millennials-dependency-on-digital-ordering.

24. "How Domino's Is Winning the Pizza Wars," CNBC, July 25, 2019. Accessed at https://www.youtube.com/watch?v=FWu2rkffYvg.

25. Jonathan Maze, "How Domino's Became a Tech Company."

Chapter 15

1. John Ellett, "Being Transparent to Revitalize a Brand—the Domino's Story," *Forbes*, August 25, 2011. Accessed at https://www

.forbes.com/sites/johnellett/2011/08/25/being-transparent
-to-revitalize-a-brand-the-dominos-story/#73ae043421ed.

2. Andrew Perrin, "Social Media Usage: 2005–2015," Pew Research Center, October 8, 2015. Accessed at https://www.pewresearch .org/internet/2015/10/08/social-networking-usage-2005-2015/.

3. Russell Weiner, presentation at Center for Entrepreneurship at the University of Michigan, December 8, 2015.

4. Edelman Trust Barometer, 2010. Accessed at https://www .edelman.com/sites/g/files/aatuss191/files/2018-10/2010 -edelman-trust-barometer-executive-summary.pdf.

5. Jeremy White, "2011 Pizza Chain of the Year—Domino's Pizza," *Pizza Today,* June 1, 2011. Accessed at https://www.pizzatoday .com/departments/features/2011-june-chain-of-the-year/.

6. Bob Garfield, "Domino's Does Itself a Disservice by Coming Clean," *Ad Age,* January 11, 2010. Accessed at https://adage.com /article/ad-review/advertising-domino-s-a-disservice-ads/141393.

7. Paul Farhi, "Behind Domino's Mea Culpa Ad Campaign," *Washington Post,* January 13, 2010. Accessed at https://www .washingtonpost.com/wp-dyn/content/article/2010/01/12 /AR2010011201696.html.

8. Adam Sternbergh, "The Art of the Apology Ad," *New Republic,* August 3, 2010. Accessed at https://newrepublic.com /article/76719/art-apology-ad-bp-toyota-dominos.

9. Steve Capp, "Domino's 'Pizza Turnaround' Represents About-Face in Marketing and Product," *DMN,* February 28, 2010. Accessed at https://www.dmnews.com/marketing-channels /social/article/13039708/dominos-pizza-turnaround-represents -aboutface-in-marketing-and-product.

10. Lizzy Alfs, "Patrick Doyle: How Domino's Pizza Used Social Media to Change Its Reputation," *Ann Arbor News,* February 21, 2013. Accessed at http://www.annarbor.com/business-review /patrick-doyle-how-dominos-pizza-used-social-media-to-change -its-reputation/.

11. KC Ifeanyi, "Domino's Fires Up the Think Oven to Tap Consumer Creativity," *Fast Company,* February 7, 2012. Accessed at https://www.fastcompany.com/1679805/domino-s-fires-up-the -think-oven-to-tap-consumer-creativity.

12. A. Guttmann, "Advertising Spending of Selected Restaurant Chains in 2018," Statista, September 25, 2019. Accessed at https://www.statista.com/statistics/261957/ad-spend-of -selected-restaurants-in-the-us/.

Chapter 16

1. Pizza Today rankings, November 1, 2017. Accessed at https:// www.pizzatoday.com/pizzeria-rankings/2017-top-100-pizza -companies/.

2. Pizza Today rankings, November 1, 2018. Accessed at https:// www.pizzatoday.com/pizzeria-rankings/2018-top-100-pizza -companies/.

3. Domino's. Accessed at https://dominos.gcs-web.com/static-files /7f6ab901-555f-44d5-a5b5-63a5608f947c.

4. "Yum! Brands' $130 Million Plan to Fix Pizza Hut," QSR, May 4, 2017. Accessed at https://www.qsrmagazine.com/news/yum -brands-130-million-plan-fix-pizza-hut.

5. "Pizza Hut's Sales Slump Is Over," QSR, November 2, 2017. Accessed at https://www.qsrmagazine.com/news/pizza-huts-sales -slump-over.

6. "Yum! Brands' $130 Million Plan to Fix Pizza Hut," QSR, May 4, 2017.

7. Jonathan Maze, "Pizza Hut's Sales Continue to Falter," Nation's Restaurant News, August 3, 2017. Accessed at https://www.nrn .com/operations/pizza-hut-sales-continue-falter.

8. Sarah Whitten, "Pizza Hut's Multi-Decade Reign in the Pizza Sector Could Come to an End in 2018," CNBC, May 17, 2017. Accessed at https://www.cnbc.com/2017/05/17/pizza-huts -multi-decade-reign-in-the-pizza-sector-could-come-to-an-end -in-2018.html.

9. Jonathan Maze, "Pizza Hut's Sales Continue to Falter."

10. Jonathan Maze, "Pizza Hut's Sales Continue to Falter."

11. Domino's. Accessed at https://dominos.gcs-web.com/static-file s/77c9b184-0d8b-4f7f-9ef5-ffb183ca6dce.

12. Pizza Hut. Accessed at http://investors.yum.com/file/Index?Key File=389752425.

13. Domino's. Accessed at https://dominos.gcs-web.com/static-files/04e01277-9e97-46ed-ab39-da06228d23fc.
14. "Pizza Hut's Sales Slump Is Over," *QSR*, November 2, 2017.
15. Domino's press release. Accessed at https://www.prnewswire.com/news-releases/dominos-pizza-announces-fourth-quarter-and-fiscal-2017-financial-results-300600986.html.
16. "Domino's Unseats Pizza Hut as Biggest Pizza Chain," *Ad Age*, February 20, 2018. Accessed at https://adage.com/node/1007286/printable/print.
17. "How Has Domino's Fared with Respect to Other Pizza Chains?" Trefis. Accessed at https://dashboards.trefis.com/no-login-required/94WMiQaR?fromforbesandarticle=dominos-pizza-inc-leads-pizza-chain-growth-across-the-world.

Chapter 17

1. 2019 Pizza Power Report, *PMQ Magazine*, December 2018. Accessed at https://www.pmq.com/the-2019-pizza-power-report-a-state-of-the-industry-analysis.
2. Domino's 2019 Investor Day presentation. Accessed at https://dominos.gcs-web.com/static-files/fbedcbc4-ac98-4b69-bcdd-40252717d02b.
3. 2019 Pizza Power Report.
4. 2019 Pizza Power Report.
5. 2019 Pizza Power Report.
6. Domino's 2019 Investor Day presentation.
7. Julie Littman, "Domino's Aims for $25 B in Retail Sales by 2025," *Retail Dive*, January 18, 2019. Accessed at https://www.restaurantdive.com/news/dominos-aims-for-25b-in-retail-sales-by-2025/546338/.
8. Nicholas Rossolillo, "Domino's Pizza Will Be Just Fine during the Delivery Wars," Motley Fool, July 20, 2019. Accessed at https://www.fool.com/investing/2019/07/20/dominos-pizza-will-be-just-fine-during-the-deliver.aspx.
9. Sarwant Singh, "The Soon to Be $200 Billion Online Food Delivery Is Rapidly Changing the Global Food Industry," *Forbes*, September 9, 2019. Accessed at https://www.forbes.com/sites

/sarwantsingh/2019/09/09/the-soon-to-be-200b-online
-food-delivery-is-rapidly-changing-the-global-food-industry
/#75e47159b1bc.

10. Sarwant Singh, "The Soon to Be $200 Billion Online Food De-
livery Is Rapidly Changing the Global Food Industry."

Business Lessons and Opportunities

1. Julie Littman, "Domino's Aims for $25 B in Retail Sales by 2025."

INDEX

THE
MICROSOFT
STORY

Available now from HarperCollins Leadership

CHAPTER ONE

THE EARLY YEARS

The future was here. Paul Allen rushed through Harvard Square to reach his friend Bill Gates to show him the January 1975 issue of *Popular Electronics,* the magazine devoted to gadgets and gizmos.

The gizmo on the cover would change computers forever—and inspire the creation of one of the world's most influential companies.

World's First Minicomputer Kit to Rival Commercial Models . . .
"Altair 8800"

The article about the Altair 8800 picked up on page thirty-three.

The era of the computer in every home—a favorite topic among science-fiction writers—has arrived! It's made possible by the POPULAR ELECTRONICS/MITS Altair 8800, a full-blown computer that can hold its own against sophisticated minicomputers now on the market. And it doesn't cost several thousand dollars. In fact, it's in a color TV-receiver's price class—under $400 for a complete kit.

The Altair 8800 is not a "demonstrator" or souped-up calculator. It is the most powerful computer ever presented as a construction project in any electronics magazine. In many ways, it represents a revolutionary development in electronic design and thinking.[1]

The computer's front panel included rows of switches and LEDs. Behind the lid, the Altair featured an 8-bit parallel processor and 65,000 words of maximum memory, along with a new LSI chip and seventy-eight basic machine instructions (as compared with forty in the usual minicomputer). "This means that you can write an extensive and detailed program," the authors wrote.[2] But someone would have to write that program. Allen and Gates thought they might be the people to do it. The pair had been teaming up ever since their days at the Lakeside School, a private boys' school in Washington State. Allen, a multifaceted dreamer, was born in 1953. Gates, a bookish, driven pragmatist, came along two years later. They both were drawn to computers and coding while attending the Lakeside School.[3] At the time, computers were massive and clunky and expensive and exclusive, generally only available to government agencies or major companies or academics in math and science disciplines.

Lakeside had a Teletype Model ASR-33 (for Automatic Send and Receive) terminal with a paper tape reader that linked over the school's phone line to a GE-635, "a General Electric mainframe computer in a distant, unknown office," Allen recalled decades later.

"The Teletype made a terrific racket, a mix of low humming, the Gatling gun of the paper-tape punch, and the *ka-chacko-whack* of the printer keys. The room's walls and ceiling had to be lined with white corkboard for soundproofing. But though it was noisy and slow, a dumb remote terminal with no display screen or lower-case letters, the ASR-33 was also state-of-the-art. I was transfixed. I sensed that you could do things with this machine."[4]

The school's Mothers Club held a rummage sale and used the proceeds to buy the Teletype and computer time on the GE computer. But computer time was expensive—whoever was using it had to be efficient and creative. "You would type the programs off-line on this yellow paper tape and then put it into the tape reader, dial up the computer, and very quickly feed in the paper tape and run your program," Gates said. "They charged you not only for the connect time, but also for storage units and CPU time. So, if you had a program that had a loop in it of some type you could spend a lot of money very quickly. And so we went through the money that the Mothers Club had given very rapidly. It was a little awkward for the teachers, because it was just students sitting there and zoom—the money was gone."[5]

The system used a computer language called BASIC that was developed in 1964 by Dartmouth College math professors John Kemeny and Thomas Kurtz (BASIC, speaking to its ambitions for widespread use, stands for Beginners' All-purpose Symbolic Instruction Code).[6] Computers needed language to run, and even if computers weren't readily available for public use, BASIC created the potential of computer programming for the masses.

Allen and Gates Meet

It was in that Teletype room, amid the Gatling gun of the paper-tape punch and *ka-chacko-whack* of the printer keys, that Paul Allen and Bill Gates first connected. The pair reflected an image of contrasts. The older Allen, with his long side-burns and stocky build, looked a decade older than the boy-ish, gaunt Gates.

Where Allen's family struggled to afford tuition but wanted to challenge him (his father was a University of Washington librarian and his mother was a schoolteacher),[7] Gates, nick-named "Trey" as a child, had been raised in a prominent family—his father was a successful lawyer and his mother was involved with the boards of nonprofits.[8]

Despite all of their differences, they also had many similarities. They both were drawn to the limitless potential of computers and felt like a wave of opportunity was approaching. Companies such as Hewlett-Packard and Intel Corporation were emerging, and developments in memory storage and word processing were on the horizon.

Something big was happening. And Allen and Gates wanted to be a part of it.

The Lakeside Programming Group

Gates and Allen joined two other students—Ric Weiland and Kent Evans—as the most consistent visitors to the computer room. The older Allen and Weiland often paired up together, and the younger Gates and Evans quickly became best friends, reading business magazines and planning their future companies.

"We were always creating funny company names and having people send us their product literature," Gates said. "Trying to think about how business worked. And in particular, looking at computer companies and what was going on with them."[9]

As the group kept burning through the Mothers Club's computer budget, a new opportunity emerged—a time-sharing company called the Computer Center Corporation, or C-Cubed, opened in Seattle and needed testers for its Digital Equipment Corporation PDP-10 computer, since its TOPS-10 operating system was known to crash.[10]

C-Cubed offered the teens unlimited free time as testers on the company's terminals. There, they began studying code and mastering different machine language such as BASIC, COBOL (Common Business-Oriented Language), and FORTRAN (Formula Translation). Computer pioneers at C-Cubed would loan Gates and the other teens system manuals and teach them about assembly code in drips and drabs. Other times, Allen and Gates would go dumpster diving through the trash to find discarded operating system listings. Gates's weight made it easier for Allen to propel him.

"It was so exciting to get a little glimpse and beginning to figure out how computers were built, and why they were expensive," Gates recalled decades later. "I certainly think that having some dimension, when you're young, that you feel a mastery of, versus the other people around you is a very positive thing."[11]

After testing of the PDP-10 was completed, C-Cubed began charging the teens for computer time. One month, Allen's charge came to $78, which would amount to more than $500 in 2019. "I know you're learning, but can't you cut back?" his father asked him.[12]

Gates and Allen tried to tap into C-Cubed's internal files in hopes of finding a free account. Instead, they got caught, and they lost their C-Cubed privileges for the summer. That fall, Allen—in exchange for free computer time—was tasked with trying to improve C-Cubed's BASIC compiler, a program that translates source code.[13]

Allen pored through the assembly code "like an apprentice watchmaker squinting at the tiny wheels to understand their interplay," he wrote, piecing the code together word by word and becoming a BASIC virtuoso.[14]

C-Cubed taught the boys another lesson in 1970 when it closed. The company never established a solid business model. There was money to be made through computers, but you couldn't fund a company on the strength of free computer time.

With C-Cubed closed, the teens branched out. Allen, then a high school senior, began spending his time at the University of Washington's graduate computer science lab. "I was a sponge, soaking up knowledge wherever I could," he said.[15] "All of us were sponges then."

That fall, a time-sharing company in Portland hired Allen and his three "colleagues"—Gates, Weiland, and Evans—to write a payroll program in COBOL, the high-level language, and the Lakeside Programming Group was born.

The project was sprawling and cumbersome. Evans and Gates did much of the heavy lifting, but after Allen and Weiland worried there wouldn't be enough work to go around, the upperclassmen decided they could take on the project alone.

"I'm sure their friends thought it was weird that we were coming around at all, and then they decide they just want to do it. So they kicked both Kent and I off the project," Gates said. "And I said, 'I think you're underestimating how hard this is. If you ask me to come back, I am going to be totally in charge of this and anything you ever asked me to do again.'"[16]

Soon enough, Allen was asking Gates to rejoin the project, and just as he said, Gates took ownership. "It was just more natural for me to be in charge," he said.

Gates had an innate ability to synthesize information quickly. When confronted with a situation, he'd rock forward and backward, forward and backward in his chair, a means of focusing and centering himself. But Gates's analytical mind couldn't help his friends secure computer access.

In March 1971, computer lab director Dr. Hellmut Golde kicked Allen and his high school friends out of the lab. Their work "has caused a number of complaints and tends to disrupt the intended use of the laboratory," Golde wrote in a letter to Allen, citing the noise level and their removal of an acoustic coupler "without leaving at least a note. Such behavior is intolerable in any environment." Allen published the letter in a 2017 LinkedIn post announcing that the university's Department of Computer Science & Engineering was being elevated to a school and would bear his name.[17]

Allen began taking classes at Washington State University that fall after graduating from Lakeside, pledging a fraternity, and playing intramural sports, while Weiland attended Stanford, majoring in electrical engineering. The youngest members of the Lakeside Programming Group, meanwhile, were tasked with solving a new problem. Their school had merged with a local all-girls school, and Lakeside's principal needed a program to organize the class schedules.

But in May of 1972, before they could begin the project, tragedy struck. Kent Evans, Gates's closest friend, was taking a mountaineering class when he slipped and fell down a slope and died. He was seventeen years old.

"It was so unexpected, so unusual," Gates said.[18]

A Strong Pair

A grieving Gates asked Allen to help him with the scheduling program, and the friends fell into a routine, working around the clock, sleeping on cots, and going to the movies for breaks.

"I was impressed by how cleanly Bill broke the job into its component parts, and especially how he 'preloaded' himself into an English class with a dozen or more girls and no other boys," Allen wrote in his memoir, *Idea Man.* "Bill and I became closer that summer. Our age gap no longer seemed to matter; we had what I call high-bandwidth communication."[19]

That high-bandwidth communication continued with their next opportunity, which involved data processing about traffic flow—Gates called the program Traf-O-Data, playing off of the term jack-o'-lantern.[20]

Allen was drawn to the potential of the microprocessor, the heart of the computer. A colleague, Paul Gilbert, helped build a machine around an Intel 8-bit 8008 microprocessor.

The pair were also enlisted for early 1973, Gates's final semester in high school, to work on a complicated software project through the aerospace company TRW that involved a PDP-10 mainframe computer.[21] Allen took a leave of absence from Washington State, while Gates received approval for a senior project. They were paid $4 an hour and worked for days at a time.

The friends didn't spend too much time sleeping. Gates, when needing an energy rush, would pour the orange powder Tang into his hand and lick it, leaving his face and hands (and computer keys) covered in orange residue.[22] As Gates was licking Tang out of his palm and working on the TRW project, he received his acceptance to Harvard University. So off to Boston he went, three thousand miles away from home and his coding cohort.

Allen and Gates talked about leaving school and starting a company, "but it was too vague and my parents wanted me to go back to school," Gates said.[23] But the conversation never really went away. They eventually started getting clients for their traffic data collection—Traf-O-Data was finally taking off! But when Washington started offering similar services to cities for free, Traf-O-Data was pretty much finished.

Gates kept suggesting that Allen should move to Boston, so Allen inquired at different companies and ended up getting a job offer from Honeywell, the engineering and aerospace company. Gates received a job offer there, too.

"Then, after I accepted the job and prepared to take another leave from Wazzu [a nickname for Washington State University], Bill changed his mind and decided to go back to Harvard," Allen wrote. "I suspected heavy pressure from his parents, who had more traditional ideas."[24]

Either way, Allen was making a move. He and his girlfriend, Rita, drove to Boston. Allen and Gates were together again.

Honeywell wasn't what Allen expected—"a big cocoon where people punched the clock as though they were working for the phone company." Bored with the job, Allen used his friend's password to hack into Harvard's operating system, Unix.

Eventually, Rita had to return to Washington and Allen was stuck in a stale job, struggling to find his next project. He'd come up with ideas and bring them up to Gates, but the technology wasn't adequate.

It would stay that way until the friends saw the Altair 8800 on the cover of *Popular Electronics*. And then they sprang into action.

Calling Their Shot

On January 2, 1975, Allen mailed a letter to MITS, or Micro Instrumentation and Telemetry Systems, the company behind the Altair 8800. "We have available a BASIC language interpreter which runs on MCS-8080 series microcomputers," Allen wrote. "We are interested in selling copies of this software to hobbyists thru you. It could be supplied on cassettes or floppy disks to users of your ALTAIR series microcomputers. We would anticipate charging you $50 a copy which you would then sell for somewhere between $75 and $100. If you are interested, please contact us."[25] They sent the letter on letterhead from Traf-O-Data, their defunct traffic data collection company.

MITS employees did not respond to the letter, so Gates called MITS, and the pair got to work. They faced multiple obstacles. Most notably, they'd be creating the interpreter without using an Altair or Intel 8080 microprocessor.

But Allen and Gates had a head start because of their work with Traf-O-Data, and they were savvy enough to recognize that they were onto something special. They saw a problem, an opportunity, a need—who else would be better suited than them? And they believed in their ability to find an answer.

Their biggest concern involved floating-point math code and the need for decimals to be in the right places in their code. As they discussed the issue at a Harvard cafeteria, a nearby student, Monte Davidoff, spoke up. "I've done those for the PDP-8," said Davidoff, who became a third member of the team.[26]

Gates handled the interpreter's programming while Davidoff tackled the math package. The team regularly pulled all-nighters, motivating and inspiring one another, driving each other to achieve something beyond themselves. "We worked all hours, with double shifts on weekends. Bill basically stopped going to class," Allen remembered.[27]

Continue Reading *The Microsoft Story*,
available now from HarperCollins Leadership

The future is within reach.

When you start making your goals a top priority, everything falls into place. Learn from the leaders inspiring millions & apply their strategies to your professional journey.

eadership
ssentials
Blog

Activate 180
Podcast

Interactive
E-courses

Free templates

gn up for our free book summaries!
spire your next head-turning idea.
eadershipessentials.com/pages/book-summaries

LEADERSHIP
ESSENTIALS
by HarperCollins Leadership

For more business and leadership advice and resources, visit hcleadershipessentials.com.

What can you learn from the **most successful** companies in the world?

Find out with
The Business Storybook Series
from HarperCollins Leadership.

Mary Curran Hackett

THE CAPITAL ONE STORY

How the Upstart Financial Institution Charged Toward Market Leadership

Stephanie and Charlie Wetzel

THE MARVEL STUDIOS STORY

How a Failing Comic Book Publisher Became a Hollywood Superhero

Rich Mintzer

THE NBA STORY

How the Sports League Slam-Dunked Its Way into a Global Business Powerhouse

Mary Curran Hackett

THE SEPHORA STORY

The Retail Success You Can't Make Up

Dan Good

THE MICROSOFT STORY

How the Tech Giant Rebooted Its Culture, Upgraded Its Strategy, and Found Success in the Cloud

Bill Chastain

THE TARGET STORY

How the Iconic Big Box Store Hit the Bullseye and Created an Addictive Retail Experience

Marcia Layton Turner

THE DOMINO'S STORY

How the Innovative Pizza Giant Used Technology to Deliver a Customer Experience Revolution

Stephanie and Charlie Wetzel

THE SPANX STORY

What's Underneath the Incredible Success of Sara Blakely's Billion Dollar Empire

Behind every business there is a story to be told:

- Learn what problem each of these companies set out to solve and how they are solving it.
- Explore which tough decisions have led to their success.
- Understand how their employees have made the company what it is today.
- Determine how you can apply the lessons from their story to your own business and career.

Find these titles at harpercollinsleadership.com/storybooks